"Greg Goode's latest book, and totally accessible, and it Path of true awakening. Sidestepping the usual esoteric double-talk that often passes for non-dual wisdom, the author provides a very specific and practical framework for deepening the direct experience of your own true nature. Highly recommended."

— **Chuck Hillig**, author of *Enlightenment for Beginners*, *The Way IT Is*, *Seeds for the Soul*, *Looking for God*, and *The Magic King*

"Greg Goode shifts fluidly between roles as educator, realized guide, and confidant. The synergy of the three voices, all coming from the disposition of 'joyful irony,' brings into being a friend who is powerful company for the investigation into what one is. Greg's treatment of ethics is groundbreaking and timely in non-dualistic literature. The chapters on witnessing awareness cover its nature and dissolution with a kind of twist regarding the final dissolution. These and other significant themes are turned by Greg into fortunate opportunities for investigators and enjoyers of non-dual literature."

— **Jerry Katz**, founder of nonduality.com and editor of *One*

"Greg Goode's *After Awareness* explores the diamond from every angle, presenting a joyful dance of spiritual perspectives and non-duality pointers. The book navigates the non-dual territory with a sense of ease and joy, profound understanding, and a freedom from attachment to paths and approaches."

— **David Rivers**, publisher of Tandava Press

After Awareness

The End of the Path

GREG GOODE

NON-DUALITY PRESS
An Imprint of New Harbinger Publications

Publisher's Note

Distributed in Canada by Raincoast Books

Copyright © 2016 by Greg Goode
        Non-Duality Press
        An imprint of New Harbinger Publications, Inc.
        5674 Shattuck Avenue
        Oakland, CA 94609
        www.newharbinger.com

Cover design by Amy Shoup

Library of Congress Cataloging-in-Publication Data on file

18   17   16

10   9   8   7   6   5   4   3   2   1   First Printing

Contents

Introduction

You may already be familiar with the term "direct path." It has been used by different spiritual teachers. But in this book I use the term to refer to the teachings inspired by Shri Atmananda Krishna Menon (1883–1959). Shri Atmananda's direct path provides a strikingly modern way to experience peace and happiness that are unruffled by circumstances.

If you're not, or if you would like a refresher, in chapter 1, "What Is the Direct Path?" I give a condensed version of the path. I describe the student's progress from beginning to end and discuss the fruits of successful inquiry. I point out how the direct path is able to disappear without a trace. I discuss various critiques of the direct path and consider the question of which path is the "highest."

This book could have been called *Secrets of the Direct Path—Revealed!* Because in it you'll read about aspects of the direct path that are rarely, if ever, written down. In this book—unlike my previous books on the subject—I'm not giving pointers or exercises to assist you in non-dual realization (apart from the condensed version mentioned above). Rather, I wish to provide you with a look at the inner workings of the direct path, to show you how the machinery does its work. My sympathetic deconstruction is written from a mixed standpoint, as though I had one foot inside the path and one foot outside. Seeing both sides of the path will allow you to look around without having to become converted, without having to believe in the truth of the path's concepts.

Why I Wrote This Book

What's so great about looking around the path in this way? Isn't it better to just stop talking and call off the search for liberation? Just rest in awareness? My answer is that many other resources can help you rest in awareness. I've written some of them myself. This particular book, however, has different purposes. Communication is a unifying theme among these purposes.

Communication

One purpose of this book is to help us find a way to talk about awareness in the twenty-first century. In fact, the topics in this book arose from twenty-first-century confrontations among different spiritual paths. What do Buddhists and physicists say about such a path, which places so much emphasis on concepts such as global awareness? These days, people from different backgrounds converse much more than they did ten or twenty years ago. In fact, most people looking for a spiritual home will shop around before settling down. They'll spend some time with a variety of offerings, such as traditional Vedanta, yoga, Western mysticism, Zen, Theravada, Tibetan Buddhism, and independent non-duality teachings. There are even online discussion groups for these kinds of inter-path interchanges.

So, how does the direct path represent itself in an open forum of that kind? How can the direct path be communicated to someone who has been around the block and seen a lot of different world-views? If someone announces, "You and the world are awareness—this can be experienced at any time," it'll fall flat in these postmodern polyglot contexts. Some paths don't agree. Some paths don't even have any notion of global awareness. If proponents of these paths hear someone say, "You are awareness," they may feel it's a dogmatic message. How can someone discuss the direct path in a mixed context without dogmatism, without coming across as if the path's concepts are supposed to be true for everyone everywhere? This seemingly specialized issue often comes up because of the mixed contexts in contemporary online forums and other arenas of discussion and inquiry. Many people use the Internet as their spiritual guide, and few people pick a path without sampling lots of other ones.

To foster open, non-dogmatic communication is one of the main purposes of this book.

Another purpose is to help clarify some issues around the direct path's "awareness" idea. Here are two real-life examples where clarification is needed.

Awareness or Consciousness?

In the direct path, the terms "awareness" and "consciousness" are synonymous. In terms of the direct path as a form of spirituality, awareness is a teaching tool shared by various Vedantic paths. It assists in the process of self-inquiry. In the context of the direct path itself, awareness is taught as the nature of the self. It's the essence of being, knowledge, and love. It's the sum and substance of all things. It doesn't stand apart and cognize things that are different from itself. For this reason, there's ultimately no duality between subject and object. Awareness is also whole. It doesn't exist in separate compartments, pools, or pockets. For this reason, there's no duality within awareness itself.

Experientially, awareness is said to have a "witnessing aspect" when your experience seems to consist of thoughts, feelings, and sensations that come and go. In this case, awareness witnesses the coming and going of objects. Awareness is that to which objects appear.

When your experience isn't characterized by comings and goings, awareness has no witnessing aspect. This is referred to as "pure consciousness," or "consciousness without objects." Through deep, experiential inquiry, the witnessing aspect becomes more and more salient and then becomes more and more subtle. Finally, the witnessing aspect collapses or fades away. This point is sometimes referred to as "non-dual realization" or "self-realization." I discuss the witnessing aspect of awareness in more detail in chapter 6, "Witnessing Awareness—Introduction."

Beyond Awareness?

In the direct path, awareness is the non-dual nature of all things. In other non-dual teachings, awareness has a less final status.

For example, several years ago, a small wave of non-dual teachers began teaching from a "beyond awareness" platform. These teachers—whose teachings were suspiciously similar, and whose new campaigns hit the Internet in the same two-week period—were promising a deep, radical truth that promised to take students further than any awareness teaching had ever gone. Within a week, I received several e-mails and even a frantic telephone call: "Greg! What *is* this teaching? What do they mean, 'beyond awareness'? There can't be anything beyond awareness as taught in the direct path, can there? *Can there?!*" My caller was worried about another teaching being higher than his! He asked me to look into it, as though giving me a non-dual detective assignment. I found that each of the teachers in question was using ideas and quotes from Nisargadatta's book *Prior to Consciousness*. No problem! The issue turned out to be semantic only. This is because "consciousness" for Nisargadatta is very different from "consciousness" or "awareness" for Shri Atmananda and the direct path. In fact, a fair equivalent would be

Prior to consciousness (Nisargadatta)

=

Pure consciousness (Atmananda).

My caller felt very relieved to hear this. He hadn't invested in a suboptimal teaching after all!

Another example that repeatedly calls for clarity happens when the direct path meets Buddhism. A few years ago, a Buddhist friend of mine became interested in the direct path. But he felt alienated by the path's heavy emphasis on awareness. It seemed to him that the emphasis on awareness represented a form of clinging, which in Buddhism represents suffering at a subtle level. So how could the direct path address this issue with the Buddhist student? I cover this point more thoroughly in the next chapter and in chapter 10, "After Awareness: The End of the Path." But my short answer to my friend was that ultimately, the direct path doesn't make any metaphysical assertions about awareness. The direct path is "eco-friendly." It cleans up after itself. It doesn't soil the environment with attachments or metaphysical clutter. Not even awareness is a lasting commitment.

Who Would Benefit from Reading This Book?

If you're a student of the direct path and feel stuck somewhere, then the open, pragmatic, and deconstructive approach taken here could loosen things up. If you find yourself in a position of communicating about awareness in a mixed forum, the set of less doctrinaire terms and pointers in this book might help.

If you aren't a student but feel interested in the direct path's methods of accomplishing its goal of freedom, then this book might help. It may give you a non-dogmatic glimpse into how a person can begin with an everyday perspective and come to find freedom from perspectives.

Overview of the Chapters

This book doesn't assume familiarity with the direct path. You can find out more about the direct path in chapter 1, "What Is the Direct Path?"

In non-dual paths, the truth is often described as love. But how do truth and love come together? My own experience is that education and teaching are essential parts of our progress toward freedom and a loving way of life, and the time-tested traditional paths agree on this. In chapter 2, "The Path and the Heart," I urge teachers, presenters, and students of non-dual paths to include some sort of ethical approach with whatever else they do to promulgate the teachings.

Very few non-dual teachings treat the issue of language head-on. Sometimes they tell us that words are pointers or fingers pointing to the moon. But the direct path takes a more sophisticated nonreferential approach that cuts through the dualisms implied by these pointers. This is the subject of chapter 3, "The Language of Joyful Irony."

In Shri Atmananda's dialogues, there's considerable emphasis on the guru. Atmananda often said that a living guru is indispensable for self-knowledge. But what if a student can't travel to see the guru—is there any hope for this student? In chapter 4, "The Guru Doctrine," I discuss this issue in a way that may provide hope for such a student.

The direct path is often associated with one particular method of investigation—self-inquiry. As important as this method is, it's not everyone's cup of tea. There are several other approaches to non-dual realization in the direct path. They include standing as awareness, guided meditations, reminders, and working with the body. Although used in retreats, they're not well-covered in the direct path's written sources. I discuss these and other alternative methods in chapter 5, "Alternatives to Inquiry."

Along with the idea of direct experience, the witness is the direct path's most prominent tool of inquiry. Over the past decade or so, I've received hundreds of questions about witnessing awareness:

"What is it? Can I see it?"

"Why don't all paths use this notion?"

"Is it like my mind?"

"Can I follow the direct path without it?"

"Is witnessing awareness a metaphysical assumption that I'm saddled with forever? And, exactly how does it dissolve at the end? Can I skip to that part now?"

I discuss these issues in great detail in chapters 8, 9, and 10.

Chapter 6, "Witnessing Awareness—Introduction," sets forth the basic notion of "witnessing awareness" used by the direct path. This chapter discusses how the direct path uses the witness notion as a liberating tool. In chapter 7, "The Opaque Witness," witnessing awareness is defined in a non-metaphysical way, which I hope makes some sense even for readers who don't resonate with the idea of global awareness of universal proportions. I explain why the witness isn't the same as the mind, as well as why there aren't two or more witnesses. Chapter 8, "The Transparent Witness," and chapter 9, "Non-dual Realization and the End of the Witness," cover the entire progression of the witness in considerable detail. In those chapters, I trace the growth of clarity, love, and happiness as they progress from the witness's grosser opaque phase, to its more subtle transparent phase, all the way through its eventual dissolution. When witnessing awareness dissolves, this is considered non-dual realization, or *sahaja samadhi*.

And then what? When the witness dissolves, the immediate feeling is that it dissolves into pure consciousness. In fact, this is the direct path's official teaching. But something more profound happens, which relates to freedom from the path itself. A deeply thrilling part of non-dual realization is freedom from the teaching that brought you freedom. It seems like a paradox. I refer to this freedom as "joyful irony." It bears the sweetness of openhearted love and a zest for life. In joyful irony, you find it impossible to attach or cling to the idea that what's really here is awareness. Not even Shri Atmananda proclaims that in the end it's all consciousness. This freedom from attachment, especially attachment to our own most cherished vocabulary, is what I mean by "after awareness" and "the end of the path."

CHAPTER 1

What Is the Direct Path?

If you're already familiar with the direct path, you can skip this chapter, although you might find it a useful refresher.

In this book, "the direct path" refers to the teachings inspired by Shri Atmananda Krishna Menon. I've written two books on the direct path: *Standing as Awareness: The Direct Path* (Non-Duality Press, 2009) and *The Direct Path: A User Guide* (Non-Duality Press, 2012). These books present the path in a patient, experiential way. With *Standing as Awareness: The Direct Path*, you get a bird's-eye view of the direct path and the liberation that is its goal. On the other hand, *The Direct Path: A User Guide* unfolds the teachings in a logical sequence. It also contains guided investigations, which allow you to experience the insights leading to non-dual realization.

The direct path places much emphasis on inquiry and investigation, but there are also other methods employed by the direct path, such as reminders, the Heart Opener, and the Yoga of Awareness. In chapter 5, "Alternatives to Inquiry," I discuss these methods in greater detail than you'll find in either Shri Atmananda's published material or my previous books.

Background

The term "direct path" was used by Ramana Maharshi as early as the 1920s.[1] In fact, in the teachings of both Ramana Maharshi and

Shri Atmananda, the direct path is a form of inquiry derived from traditional Vedanta that doesn't take the long-established road of good works, religious rituals, devotion to deities, ascetic purification, and belief in cosmological theories. But over the years, in the West, the term "direct path" has come to be associated more with Shri Atmananda than with Ramana Maharshi. Besides Shri Atmananda, well-known expositors of the direct path include Jean Klein, John Levy, Wolter Keers, Ananda Wood, Francis Lucille, Philip Renard, and Rupert Spira.

The primary method of investigation used in the direct path is *atma vichara*, or self-inquiry, in which you look at aspects of the world, the body, and the mind, trying to find any location where the self could possibly reside. You also try to find anything truly separate from yourself as witnessing awareness.

We normally feel separate from things in the world, from people and things we love. We even feel separate from aspects of our own body and mind! The sense of separation makes us feel lonely and vulnerable. We feel subject to finitude, suffering, and death. But when you deeply realize that nothing finite is the self, and that there's no experiential basis for separation, you discover your natural wholeness. You discover clarity, sweetness, and joy—all of which become your living experience.

Awareness

In the direct path, awareness refers to an open, global clarity. If we add the function of "being appeared to" as an overlay on top of awareness, the result would be "witnessing awareness." Witnessing awareness, as I discuss in chapters 7, 8, and 9, is characterized as "that to which appearances appear" or "the unseen seer."

Awareness isn't mental or physical. It's that to which the body and the mind appear. In the direct path, you can come to see how the body and the mind *appear to* awareness, rather than being *perceived by* awareness. This seeing is crucial in the direct path, and there are many experiments that facilitate it.

Of course, we normally attribute such seeing to the individual person. We think the person is the seer. We think that whatever appears, appears to that person. We think that physical objects are perceived by the senses and that abstract objects are cognized by the mind. Normally we aren't so interested in what sees the senses or how the mind itself is perceived. But in the direct path, you examine the full range of experience, including what seems to be the very equipment that conveys experience to you.

As you inquire about the body and the mind, you feel your perspective broadening, as though you're zooming out further and further. It's not that you're becoming omniscient but that your perspective is loosening. The "I" seems less and less associated with the body. The "I" seems more and more like awareness itself.

As you continue with your inquiry, you realize that awareness isn't the same thing as biological sentience. Sentience is usually defined as an organism's capacity to perceive, feel, and respond to conditions. It's a biological function. It depends on the health of the organism, and it may come and go in various states of wakefulness, sleep, trance, and coma. Awareness, on the other hand, transcends the organism. It's that to which these states appear. According to the direct path, sentience is an object—as are, for instance, color or sound.

Some spiritual paths distinguish between awareness and consciousness. Although the direct path distinguishes awareness from sentience, it considers awareness and consciousness the same thing. For a more detailed treatment of awareness and similar concepts, see "How the Direct Path Sees Witnessing Awareness" in chapter 6, "Witnessing Awareness—Introduction."

About Self-Inquiry

In the direct path, self-inquiry is your main tool for investigating the world, the body, and the mind. *What's the true nature of the mind? Is my body my self? Is the world separate from the seeing of the world?*

Your investigation encompasses the entire range of experience, including thoughts, feelings, beliefs, sensations, emotions, intuitions, and states of mind. Are they separate and objectively existing things? They certainly seem to be. In our everyday ways of thinking, feeling, and speaking, we certainly treat the world, the body, and the mind as separate. There are even philosophies and sciences that argue that they truly are separate.

But if you look very closely for these supposedly separate things, can you actually find them? Does your experience verify separateness? With self-inquiry, you find just the opposite. You never confirm true separateness, no matter what you examine. Whatever you inquire into is confirmed to be your self, the "Self" of awareness.

Self-inquiry uses two investigative tools: witnessing awareness and direct experience.

Witnessing Awareness

Witnessing awareness is awareness in its aspect of being the subject of appearing objects. Whatever you examine—whether it be a piece of fruit, your lower back, or your most sublime mental state—appears to witnessing awareness. Your thoughts, feelings, and sensations appear to witnessing awareness. Yet witnessing awareness doesn't appear to anything. It isn't an object. It has no color, size, shape, or duration. Unlike the mind, witnessing awareness doesn't come and go. It doesn't grow sluggish when you're tired. It doesn't become active when you drink coffee. It doesn't shut off if you go into a coma. It doesn't suffer. Witnessing awareness is that to which the coming and going of sentience appears. This idea takes some getting used to, and there are many methods in the direct path to help you attune to it. You grow to be able to see witnessing awareness as the home of direct experience.

Direct Experience

Direct experience is the other principal investigative tool in the direct path. What is direct experience? It's a kind of experience that's not the result of inference or interpretation.

In the direct path, if you examine a table to discover its true nature, you don't begin by assuming that the table exists in front of you. You examine your experience to ascertain what does appear. In your visual experience of the table, if it seems that "the table's brown color" appears, then this experience is the result of an inference. Really, there's no evidence that the brown color belongs to a table. In your visual experience, nothing establishes that the color comes from a table. A *thought* may make such a claim (and thoughts are examined later on in this book), but in the visual data itself, there's nothing that proves that a table caused the evidence. If your experience seems to be something raw and non-conceptual, something preverbal and simpler than a belief, then this is closer to a direct, non-inferential experience. A more direct rendition of your experience in this example would be "brown" or "color." Even though these are still labels, they don't make existential claims that something exists in front of you.

The direct path's emphasis on direct experience is a way to give more attention to the senses and bodily sensations, which are often overlooked in non-dual paths. But direct experience is also used when looking at the mind and conceptuality. Let's say you believe that thoughts come from the subconscious mind. When you experience a thought, what's actually showing up in your direct experience? Perhaps a quietness, followed by a thought, followed by quietness. Do you at any time directly experience an actual subconscious mind giving rise to the thought? If not, then you can't conclude that you're directly experiencing such a thing as the subconscious mind. With that insight, you suddenly begin to feel more whole and integrated.

An Example of Inquiry

Here's an example of self-inquiry that you can do in the early stages of the direct path. There are many similar inquiries in *The Direct Path: A User Guide*. The goal of doing such inquiries is to discover whether your everyday view of the world as objective and separate is validated by your direct experience.

Our sense of feeling separate from things is based on our beliefs that these things exist in a separate and independent way. We feel that we ourselves exist like this too. This usually manifests in the feeling that things are *out there* and we are *in here*. We feel the need to reach out and make contact with some things and avoid contact with other things. Because we feel separate, we feel that we need the right sorts of contact with things or people "out there" in order to support and defend ourselves. Our many failures along these lines cause us to experience a great deal of suffering.

But are these feelings of separation verified by direct experience? In this inquiry, you test for the truth of these beliefs of separation by examining a physical object: a clock.

If this clock really exists in the independent, objective way that most people feel it does, then your inquiry should be able to verify this independence. So you take a close look. What if you find wholeness instead of separation? Then perhaps you can glimpse another way of experiencing the world. You may discover that we don't need to believe in the separation that we so often assume exists. You may discover that we don't need to suffer.

The inquiry proceeds in stages, having you look closer and closer. Following your best sensory evidence, you look for anything that might independently establish that the clock exists apart from awareness. Begin by positioning yourself comfortably near a clock with a pendulum or an audible second hand. Relax so that you feel at ease. Notice that you can tune in to the simple sense of being present. Dwell on that sense for a few minutes.

Inquiry Part 1—Do you find a clock in the sound?

1. **Allow your eyes to close gently.**

2. **Listen to the sound.** "Tick tock tick tock tick tock tick tock."

3. **Focus on the *tick tock*.** Attune to the sound itself. Ignore any explanatory thoughts about what must be creating the sound.

4. **Try to find the clock.** Going just by the *tick-tock* sound, do you find a clock present? Is there any direct experience of a clock in the sound? Does the sound come self-labeled as originating from a clock? Do you find a clock *hidden* in the sound? Do you find a clock *beyond* the sound? In your direct experience of the sound, do you find any evidence that the sound is caused by a clock?

5. **Allow your eyes to open.**

These steps establish that in your direct experience of the *tick-tock* sound, there's no clock to be found. You'll never be able to find an objectively existent clock, no matter how you try. It turns out that what you experience is nothing other than witnessing awareness.

Inquiry Part 2—Do you actually hear a sound?

This part of the inquiry is more subtle. It asks the same question about the sound that part 1 asked about the clock. If you go by your sense of hearing, do you find the sound to be something that's objectively present? Normally we think of sounds as being picked up by our sense of hearing. We theorize that these sounds are the same thing as vibrations in the air that travel from objects to organisms. That is, we think of sounds as existing objectively, whether we hear them or not. When we hear the sounds, we think that they were already there, only now they've come into the "range" of our hearing. But is this true? Can we verify it through direct experience?

1. **Allow your eyes to close gently.**

2. **Focus on the experience of the *tick-tock* sound.** Set aside ideas or theories about what must be going on. Attune to the sounds themselves.

3. **Try to find a sound.** Going by auditory evidence alone, do you directly experience a sound apart from your sense of

hearing? Do you experience a sound getting closer to your range of hearing before you actually hear it? Do you experience a sound after you hear it? Do you experience an unheard sound of any kind? Going by auditory evidence alone, do you experience a sound being the same thing as vibrating molecules? Do you experience sound appearing with a label that says, "Hi, I'm really a vibration"?

4. **Allow your eyes to open.**

These steps establish something that seems completely bizarre! You discover that in your direct experience of hearing, you don't really find a sound that enters into your sense of hearing.

In our everyday way of thinking, we visualize sound as something preexisting that moves closer to our auditory range. It exists before and after we hear it. As it gets closer, it gets louder. As it gets more distant, it gets smaller, quieter. But what we're doing with this kind of visualization is confusing the sound with a physical object that *causes* the sound. Or we visualize the sound as a set of moving sound waves.

But going by our sense of hearing, we don't experience moving objects or waves. We don't observe anything that's not heard, then partially heard, then fully heard. That's what to "hear a sound" would truly mean. We don't have any non-auditory evidence that establishes that a sound is about to be heard. Our sense of hearing isn't meeting a sound. A sound isn't coming into contact with our sense of hearing. We have no experience of the objective existence of the sound. It's not like kicking a ball, which in the everyday sense we say exists before our foot comes into contact with it. This objectivist way of thinking isn't supported by our direct experience of hearing.

Inquiry Part 3—Do you find the sense of hearing?

In this part of the inquiry, you zero in even closer. In part 1, you discovered that there's no clock to be found in the sound. The clock is nothing other than sound. In part 2, you found that there's no sound to be found in the experience of hearing. Sound is nothing other than hearing. And now we ask, "Do we even find the sense of hearing?" You'll discover that there's no hearing without witnessing awareness.

Tune in to your direct experience.

1. **Allow your eyes to close gently, or keep them open if you wish.**

2. **Tune in to your sense of hearing.** Notice how hearing is something that seems available to you. (In this part of the inquiry, it doesn't matter what the particular sounds are. Try to notice hearing itself.)

3. **Try to find your sense of hearing.** Can you find hearing apart from its appearance to witnessing awareness? Is "hearing" something that exists objectively the way you think of a table or a chair? Do you experience unexperienced hearing, which then emerges into experience? Does your sense of hearing appear with an announcement that says, "I am here, whether or not I appear to awareness"?

It's simply not our direct experience that hearing hears sounds. It's more accurate to say that what we call "hearing" is just the appearance of sound. Sound and hearing come to be the same thing. It's not the case that one of them operates on the other. We never experience sound to be separate and apart from the sense of hearing.

What the Inquiries Establish

The direct path starts with inquiry into what seem to be physical objects because they serve as our paradigm for objectivity, truth, and separation. We even tend to think that we ourselves are a physical object: the body. We also think of the mind along similar physicalist lines, as if it were a subtle container for thoughts, feelings, and memories. So if you can begin to see that physical objects can't be found in the separate, objective way we imagine, then you'll be granted the beginnings of a vaster, more liberating experience of things. You'll see that you can't possibly be the body. You can't be in the body or limited by the body. These insights will be easier and more powerful when you inquire further into the mind, into feelings, and into conceptuality.

The inquiry above used hearing, but in the direct path you do inquiries for all the senses, as well as for thought, feeling, and intuition. You can inquire into anything and everything from the world of experience. In the direct path, this includes the body, the mind, and conceptual objects as well. Just as you discovered with the clock, direct experience never verifies the separate existence of any part of the experiential world. (If you think *So what? Do these inquiries prove that things don't exist* outside *of experience?* you can examine that notion as well.[2]) What you discover instead of any kind of separate existence is the wholeness of witnessing awareness—the unity of experienced and experiencer.

The Fruits of Inquiry

You become happier, freer, and more loving as you continue to expand the range of your self-inquiry. It becomes ever clearer that you're being held in the arms of love. Your identity isn't in danger. You're not perishable. Your home isn't the body or the mind. All of your experience begins to take on a lighter, sweeter, and more expansive feeling.

Every possible candidate for your "self," you discover, is a coming-and-going object that appears to you as witnessing awareness. Your sense of identification with those passing physical or mental objects diminishes. You discover that there's no permanence, safety, or certainty in mere beliefs. You begin to realize in a deep and non-conceptual way that there's nothing else you can be but the clarity to which all this has appeared. There's earth-shattering relief, heart-rending love, and even giddy happiness in this discovery.

Self-Inquiry Isn't Performed by the Mind

Just what is it that's conducting the self-inquiry? According to the direct path, self-inquiry isn't a function of the mind. It's done from a transcendent perspective, a form of witnessing inquiry called "higher reasoning." Higher reasoning happens at the level of awareness itself, which is beyond the mind. This is why it has the ability to inquire into the mind and other objects.

There are two reasons why the mind can't inquire into the mind. One is the familiar non-dual insight that we can't see the ground we're standing on. A knife can't cut itself. An eye can't see itself. The other reason why the mind can't inquire into the mind is that it can't inquire into *anything*. This is because the mind is an arising object, and an object doesn't have the ability to investigate. Rather, investigation is attributed to the mind by a thought. In other words, it's only a thought that claims that the mind is doing things. In our direct experience, we don't observe the mind actually performing any actions or conducting any investigation. We find thoughts that *say* so, but we don't find any true referents to these thoughts. Making these discoveries about the mind is partly how we're able to see that we're not the mind. The mind isn't the nature of what we are. We're beyond the mind. Later in this book, I discuss how the direct path's investigation transcends the mind.

From Gross to Subtle to Awareness and Beyond

In the direct path, using self-inquiry, you look into the entire spectrum of experience, from the gross to the subtle. You investigate the world, then the body, then the mind. This process also includes looking into other people. Sometimes other people can seem like part of the world, and sometimes they can feel like part of your own mind. But the inquiry doesn't skip over anything. The body gets special attention. Beginning with the teachings of French spiritual teacher Jean Klein and those influenced by him, the direct path began to give a great deal of attention to the body. The body receives its own inquiry, as well as exploration through various kinds of yoga and visualization.

There are several pragmatic reasons for beginning with the gross aspects of experience and ending with the subtle. I examine these reasons in detail in chapter 6, "Witnessing Awareness— Introduction." The particular order of investigation was laid down by Shri Atmananda and called *tattvopadesha* ("teaching on reality"), the logically connected exposition of the truth.[3]

Shri Atmananda's most profound texts, *Atma Darshan* and *Atma Nirvriti*,[4] contain several passages that discuss realizing all aspects of experience and finding it to be nothing other than awareness. The general sequence goes like this:

1. We never experience an object apart from its appearance to us.

2. We never experience an appearance apart from the awareness to which appearance appears.

3. Our only experience is experience itself, which is awareness, our very self.[5]

These are abstract statements, but they form the core of the direct path's results when it looks into objects. They're like generalizations of your discoveries when you inquired into the ticking clock.

As you continue with your direct-path investigation, your perspective shifts. Your understanding clarifies. At the beginning, your sense of identity may have been linked to the body. As your investigation proceeds, you come to see how awareness is your identity. You may still think that awareness has memories, goals, and intentions, but at least it's no longer so personal. As you continue even further, your understanding clarifies even more. You come to see that the mental and psychological properties you were attributing to awareness are actually not built *into* it as properties; they're only objects that appear *to* awareness. This is referred to as moving from the opaque witness to the transparent witness.

When it no longer seems that any objects reside on their own—either inside of or outside of awareness—the witness is transparent. The witness then begins to dissolve. This happens on its own and may be preceded by increased peace, sweetness, love, and freedom.

After that point, you can remind yourself of the insights and discoveries if you wish, but there's nothing more you need to do. Your head is in the tiger's mouth. When it no longer seems that things are objects appearing to awareness at all, the witness has dissolved. This is what the direct path considers non-dual realization.

Non-dual realization is the end of the gestalt in which you experience arising/falling, coming/going, subject/object, or separation of any kind. Even though the transparent witness phase was like smoothly flowing sweet water, the dissolution of the witness is unimaginably sweeter and more indescribable. I discuss the progress of the witness in much greater detail in chapter 7, "The Opaque Witness," and chapter 8, "The Transparent Witness." The freedom involved in this non-dual realization includes freedom from attachment to the direct path, its vocabulary, its concepts, and its teaching tools. You may still value and honor these tools, but you don't regard them as objectively real or true. Their status is no more elevated than that of the elements of any other path.

I haven't seen much discussion in other direct-path works about this freedom from conceptual views. But I've written about it several times and given it the name "joyful irony." Joyful irony can be found in many systems in addition to the direct path. In my experience, even this freedom by itself is heart opening, mind-expanding, thrilling, and exhilarating. I discuss joyful irony further in chapter 3, "The Language of Joyful Irony," and chapter 10, "After Awareness: The End of the Path."

The Direct Path's Unmentioned Irony

The word "direct" gains meaning from comparison with "progressive." Direct paths and progressive paths are two different kinds of spiritual undertakings. With progressive paths, the goal is to change the body, the mind, the emotions, or the quality of experience through spiritual practices. Practices may include good works and selfless service, chanting, singing and prayers, hatha yoga, visualizations, and mental stabilization exercises. The criteria for success may include the disappearance or absorption of the separate self, as well as the diminution of mental and spiritual afflictions. Afflictions may include selfishness, aversion, anger, attachment, and indignation.

On the other hand, direct paths don't require you to change any of these subjective qualities. Direct paths focus on something else: a deep, intuitive insight into the illusory nature of the personal self to whom these qualities supposedly belong. In the direct path as taught by Shri Atmananda (and thus in this book), recognition is global: when you recognize the nature of the self, you thereby recognize the nature of the world, the body, the mind, and the mind's qualities.

The difference between progressive and direct paths can be illustrated by the famous stanzas from Zen's Platform Sutra. According to the sutra, when the Fifth Zen Patriarch was looking for a successor, he sponsored a writing contest. Monks were invited to submit verses displaying their highest understanding of dhàrma. The best verse would win successorship for its author. The head monk was favored to win. He wrote,[6]

The body is the Bodhi tree,
The mind is like a clear mirror.
At all times we must strive to polish it,
And must not let the dust collect.

While all this was going on, Hui-neng was working as a laborer at the monastery. He was an uneducated man, but he had already awakened spontaneously after hearing the Diamond Sutra. While working, he happened to hear the head monk's verse being recited. He knew that the author hadn't discovered his own nature. So Hui-neng composed a verse in reply:

Bodhi originally has no tree,

The mirror also has no stand.

Buddha nature is always clean and pure;

Where is there room for dust?

The Fifth Patriarch recognized Hui-neng's deep wisdom from this verse. And so Hui-neng eventually became the Sixth Patriarch.

These verses relate to the difference between progressive and direct paths. The work in a progressive path can be likened to polishing a mirror. The mind does become more peaceful, but the process requires endless monitoring and vigilance. The criterion of success is mind based—it's a matter of having more peaceful mental contents.

Direct paths, on the other hand, can be likened to inquiring into the nature of the mirror. The peace that comes from discovering the non-reality of the mirror is effortless and requires no vigilance or maintenance. The criterion of success is a radical change in perspective. The self and its mind become a non-issue.

Even in the direct path as taught by Shri Atmananda, there is an oft-unreported irony. That is, sometimes practices recommended in progressive paths actually make it easier to do the self-inquiry of the direct path! This is because self-inquiry requires a certain amount of concentration, patience, and peace of mind. These are the exact qualities produced by progressive-path practices! So, even though you don't need to meditate and calm the mind in order to become enlightened from the perspective of the direct path, you may find it helps you go deeper with self-inquiry!

The Tools Are Not Forever

The tools of the direct path include self-inquiry, witnessing awareness, direct experience, and higher reasoning. These are only conveniences that help you proceed along the direct path. You don't grasp or cling to them, and eventually you realize that they too are passing objects. In fact, by the time you come to the end of the direct path, even awareness ends up not being a lasting commitment or a true reality. I discuss the self-deconstruction of the path's tools in chapter 9, "Non-dual Realization and the End of the Witness," and chapter 10, "After Awareness: The End of the Path."

Critiques of the Direct Path

In my years of teaching and talking about the direct path, I've encountered two main critiques. One critique objects to the emphasis on global awareness. I'll call this the "anti-awareness" critique. Some people simply have no intuition of a greater luminous wholeness that lies beneath the surface of things. Or if they do, they don't think of it as awareness. Critics often regard the direct path's emphasis on awareness as a metaphysical attachment to something for which there's no evidence.

The other critique says that the direct path overlooks the possibility that there still might be an objective world. I'll call this the "realist" critique. This critique says: "Maybe there is an objective world beyond awareness and maybe there isn't. We just don't know." In other words, it says that the direct path's conclusions based on direct experience claim too much. The direct path gives us no right to conclude that there's no objective world. In a nutshell, this critique says, "Just because there's nothing objective in our direct experience doesn't mean that nothing objective actually exists."

Responding to these critiques is one of my main reasons for writing this book. As a joyful ironist, I can't disagree with the spirit of the anti-awareness critique. Not everyone resonates with the idea of awareness or thinks it makes sense, and resonance and intuitive affinity with the concepts can be more important than metaphysical arguments when selecting a spiritual path. I don't regard the direct path as an empirical theory that tries to report accurately what's going on with the world. Rather, I regard it as a sound, practical method that works for people whose intuitions match its guiding vision. There are many other teachings that resonate with people of different intuitions.

I disagree, however, with the anti-awareness critique's charge that the emphasis the direct path places on awareness is an attachment. I don't find it to be an attachment. At a certain point in the direct path, any metaphysical commitment to the teaching dissolves. When you investigate the world of experience deeply, your metaphysical yearning for a path-independent truth about what's "really" going on with reality becomes pacified. This metaphysical yearning is a kind of impulse that pressures us to see things as being a certain way and can cause attachment to the idea of awareness. This metaphysical impulse dissolves at the end of the teaching. For more insight into how this happens, see chapter 10, "After Awareness: The End of the Path."

The realist critique is more serious. It accuses the direct path of brushing aside the possibility of an objective world. The idea behind this critique is that awareness is its own arena, with only a limited range. Certain phenomena might appear within this range. But there might be phenomena outside this range too. What happens on the inside can't provide us with a conclusive statement about what exists on the outside. This is similar to what we say about the mind. We say that the mind can't know for sure what happens outside of itself. The best it can do is create hypotheses from appearances that happen within the mind. But it can never prove these hypotheses conclusively.

This critique goes to the heart of the direct path's teachings. It accuses the direct path of overreaching, perhaps of being mistaken at a very deep level. It's saying that students of the direct path could be deluding themselves and claiming that nothing exists. But the realist critique suffers from two misunderstandings about the direct path.

One misunderstanding assumes that the direct path conceptualizes awareness as if it were a mind, only bigger. But the direct path doesn't have you think about awareness in that way. Sure, there are some similarities: for example, both the everyday view of the mind upon which the realist critique relies and the direct path's notion of witnessing awareness are the seat of the "I" in their respective systems. They're both what appearances appear to.

But the similarities between the mind and awareness end there. The mind is limited in several ways that don't apply to awareness as taught in the direct path. For example, the mind is usually associated with a brain or a body of some sort. But in the direct path, awareness isn't tied to any phenomenon at all. The direct path doesn't take the kind of materialist approach that says that the mind is the brain, or that awareness is produced by brain activity. According to the direct path, the brain and the mind are conceptual objects that appear to awareness. The mind is said to be one of many minds that exist. But awareness is non-dual, not multiple.

The realist critique also depends on a notion of awareness as a container of content. This kind of idea about awareness has been termed "the container metaphor."[7] Being a container is fine for a can of soup, but it's not a helpful analogy for awareness. Awareness isn't a physical object and has no border between an inside and an outside. In fact, the container metaphor gets special attention in the direct path. You investigate it and find that it doesn't make any sense. You discover that there's no experiential basis for a belief in ideas such as objective existence beyond awareness.

The realist critique's other misunderstanding is based in the goals it attributes to the direct path. The direct path doesn't have those goals. The direct path doesn't attempt to make empirical, objective claims about the existence of objects. It's not saying, "I have searched the entire region outside of awareness, and I can assure you there's nothing out there."

Instead, the direct path says that if we go by experience, there's no basis for the various dualisms and separations, such as inside of awareness versus outside of awareness, self versus other, subject versus object, existence versus non-existence, separation versus togetherness, and happiness versus unhappiness. These dualisms seem convincing from the perspective of being a person, and they make us suffer. The direct path shows us that if we follow experience, we don't need to believe these dualities. We don't need to suffer. The realist critique is further discussed in chapter 6, "Witnessing Awareness—Introduction."

The direct path doesn't seek to devalue the vocabulary of the mind or the body. If you're a psychotherapist or neurologist, the direct path doesn't ask you to find different employment or require you to abandon conceptual vocabularies that speak of minds, brains, or perceptual objects. As you study the direct path, however, you may come to think of those professional vocabularies differently. You may even come up with creative new approaches in your field!

The Direct Path Is Flexible

Sometimes teachers of the direct path speak in different ways about the same things. In books, meetings, or videos, sometimes you'll hear "The world is seen through," but then you'll hear "There is no world." Or you'll hear a lot of talk about the witness, but then you'll hear that the witness dissolves. Or, as part of an experiment (as in chapter 6), you'll be told to place an orange on the table. And then you'll be invited to discover that no orange can be found!

What's going on? Do these things exist or not? Why the inconsistencies? Is there a stable language that we can rely on to be consistently true across all these situations?

The direct path, like other paths, isn't trying to create a mirror image of the world and report on things using accurate labels. Instead, it's designed to be in affinity with the student. It works with the student's own concepts and perspectives in order to provide freedom from attachment. The student's concepts and perspectives change over time, and so does the direct-path language that addresses it. The direct path isn't alone in this regard. Other paths of inquiry, such as traditional Advaita Vedanta and Prasangika Madhyamika, employ flexibility in a similar way.

For example, in the beginning, you think that the orange really exists. It really seems to be out there, separate from you. You also feel as if you're "in here," perhaps inside the body. You feel separate from the orange and the rest of the world.

But this changes as you investigate. At some point, it doesn't feel as if the orange is separate anymore. But other things feel separate, such as the power of choice or attention, or the standard of excellence for judging spiritual paths. And then at some point it doesn't feel as if these are separate. It may feel as if only arisings are separate. Things get more subtle, and your sense of separation diminishes accordingly. The language of the direct path is sensitive to these changes. It's sensitive to the way you think and communicate as a student. It tries to meet you where you are, not where it's trying to push you. One of the benefits of this sensitivity is that the direct path doesn't prescribe an official "non-dual" way of talking. This gives you a great deal of freedom as a student and communicator.

Sometimes teachers of non-dual paths talk about the "relative level" and the "absolute level." The direct path takes a considerably more nuanced approach to communication. Although it occasionally speaks in terms of these levels of reality, it speaks more often about perspectives. And there are many more than two perspectives. It's helpful to see the path as a developmental, temporal process, always in flux. As a student, you change as you go. Each time your understanding becomes clearer, your perspective shifts, even if just a little. In these shifts, also called "sublations," your previous model of the world is deconstructed into a simpler, more non-dual model. These sublations continue until you've reached freedom from models altogether. Some of the shifting language in the direct path has to do with meeting you where you are in terms of these sublations.

Another part of the shifting language in the direct path has to do with the rhetorical flexibility that all languages have. Let's say a book about the direct path tells you to begin an experiment by placing an orange on the table. So you go get an orange. You place it on the table so that you can do the experiment. Then the steps in the experiment lead you through several stages. With the help of these steps, you see that in your direct experience, no orange can be found and that the only thing in evidence is awareness itself. The author of the experiment didn't have to believe the orange truly exists in order to be able to write the experiment. The steps of the experiment aren't trying to contradict or falsify the setup instructions. It's just that they use language in different ways.

You could see this as a rhetorical register shift. The setup instructions are communicating in the rhetoric of an instructor who deals in the vocabulary of everyday objects such as tables, chairs, and the student's bodily position. The instructions aren't meant to imply that any of these items truly exist. As you read a bit further, a register shift happens. The steps in the experiment use a different vocabulary, one that helps you attune to your direct experience.

These register shifts are a natural part of language itself. Also, the direct path takes a self-aware, nonreferential approach to language. In the direct path, language is used in a way that doesn't entail the truly separate existence of anything. In fact, I wrote this entire book in the mode of joyful irony. For more about these topics, see chapter 3, "The Language of Joyful Irony," and chapter 10, "After Awareness: The End of the Path."

Which Path Is the "Highest"?

As a student inquiring into the direct path, you may want to know which is the best and highest path. You may feel sure that there *is* a best and highest. You don't want to follow the wrong path and end up in the wrong place. You don't even want to end up in a second-best place. Thus you may feel as though you should perform your due diligence and settle this issue before you get started.

The direct path doesn't argue that it's the best or quickest or truest path. It doesn't critique other paths. It doesn't say that they're wrong if they disagree about the idea of witnessing awareness. Instead, the direct path leaves it up to you, the student. If you feel an intuitive connection to the idea of a brilliant, loving clarity that unifies things, then this may attract you to the direct path. But if you don't feel this intuitive connection, you'll most likely encounter other paths that resonate more deeply with your experience, and the direct path won't consider you wrong or misguided for going a different way. If you ask in all seriousness about the highest path, a teacher of the direct path may say that paths are tools, and the most effective path is the one you resonate with the most. The same teacher might say that paths are nothing more than arisings in awareness.

But these responses probably won't hit the spot if there's a deep yearning behind your question. You may feel *sure* that there's a best path. Reality must have an optimal description, mustn't it? You may want someone to direct you to the optimal path, not to give you lukewarm, evasive, or relativistic answers. If there's a best path, you want to know about it, whether you resonate with it or not. You want the highest, maximal enlightenment.

The question about which path is best gets its force from various objectivist assumptions people already have about experience and reality. They assume that spiritual attainment is a fixed quantity that can be measured as if it were a vertical distance (the "highest" path). They also assume that there's an independent standard of preeminent excellence that would decide in favor of one path over all others.

These objectivist assumptions aren't about rocks and trees but about subtle objects such as language, states, and standards of truth. As objectivist assumptions, they're perfectly analogous to broad assumptions about the existence of the world, the body, and the mind. The direct path doesn't grant the truth of these assumptions and point out the objectively best path. Instead, it invites you to look at the assumptions behind the question. The assumptions presume that things truly exist outside of awareness. The direct path helps you look into this presumption and discover that it makes no sense.

Another way to look at this is as a play of concepts. The idea of a best path is a concept. When you discover that concepts and their purported referents are unfindable in your direct experience, then any questions you have about the best path subside into peace, harmony, and contentment.

CHAPTER 2

The Path and the Heart

King: Venerable teacher, I have summoned you here to teach
me non-dualism.

Teacher: Very well, Your Majesty. But first, please allow me to
teach you compassion.

King: I want to learn non-dualism first, then compassion.

Teacher: Your Majesty, I heard that you weren't happy with
your previous teacher and that you had him put to
death. If I teach you non-dualism first, you might do
the same to me. And then you wouldn't have the
opportunity to learn compassion. But if I am able
to teach you compassion first, you will learn both.

How should we treat others? Non-dual teachings, particularly
Western versions, haven't said much about the matter. In this
chapter, I explore ethics, altruism, and compassion in the context of
the direct path. But this is an exploration only—I have no final
answers or prescriptions. The topic is rich enough to fill a small
library, and I'd simply like to open lines of discussion so that we all
may further integrate ethics into our lives. As I said, this is only an
exploration.

I believe that non-dual teachings should say more about some
sort of kindness, respect, and love. Some of my reflections are highly
personal, because engagement with ethics is an individual matter.

This chapter is based on my experiences around ethics that I've found helpful with non-dual inquiry. I explore several reasons in favor of including such ethical topics in non-dual teachings. I also examine the strongest popular arguments *against* the inclusion of ethics in non-dual teachings.

It's not too soon to talk seriously about ethics and non-duality. The non-dual community is more mature and experienced with non-dual teachings than it was in the late 1980s, when the teachings were new and exotic in the West. Even though the question of ethics comes up easily enough when we hear of scandals involving gurus, there's wide disagreement about whether ethics should be integrated into non-dual teachings and, if so, how. I'm voting yes on "whether," but I have no general answer on "how." I just feel as though it's time to talk about it.

How Can There Be Conduct Toward Others When There Are No Others?

I consider the question of *how to treat others* a different issue from the typical non-dual question "*Are* there others?" (I investigate this in chapter 7, "The Opaque Witness.") I'm in favor of embracing kindness toward others, even if non-dual investigation reveals that there are no separate others and no personal self. There are several reasons why. One reason is that the no-separate-existence question is global, and it isn't restricted to persons. In the beginning of the non-dual path, everything—persons, tables, chairs, homes, and monthly bills—seems to exist in an independent, separate way. But as you proceed, this global sense of separation diminishes. Even though non-dual investigation reveals that there are no truly existent others, it also reveals that there are no tables, chairs, homes, or monthly bills. Everything is on a par in this way. Realizing the truth of things, you can continue to treat tables, chairs, homes, and monthly bills as if they exist, but in a joyfully ironic way (see chapter 3). There's just as much reason to treat others well.

Another reason I consider the question of how to treat others to be separate from the question about the actual existence of others is this: at the beginning and middle stages of the direct path, it certainly *seems* as though there are others, even if you want to believe that there aren't. I've even heard non-dualist students claim that there are no others and yet sooner or later complain about the poor treatment they received from another person. So why not bring a bit of Golden Rule insight into your non-dual approach and treat so-called others as you (also so-called) would like to be treated?

There's one more clarification I'd like to make before getting started. In thinking about this chapter, I wanted a term that I could use to talk about this entire issue. *What should I call the kind of teachings that I'm advocating?* In Buddhism, these teachings are about compassion. In Vedanta, they're sometimes referred to as dharmic living, and sometimes love. Western monotheistic traditions speak of *caritas:* loving your neighbor or acting as God would have you act. Ancient Greek philosophers spoke of civic virtue.

Philosophers and scholars of comparative religion use the term "ethics" as an overall label for these issues. For the purposes of this chapter, I would like to follow their lead, with one critical distinction.

The concept of ethics—even the word "ethics" itself—has an unpleasant connotation for many people. It brings up images of overbearing, dogmatic, and abusive authority figures. It may bring up memories of personal experience with rules and laws, manipulation, threats, fear, and physical punishment. Some people who grow up with dogmatic ethics end up feeling a lifelong aversion to the very idea of ethics.

In fact, many people have moved from traditional Western religions to modern non-dual paths partly because of the freedom from dogmatic ethics they perceive in non-dualism. Non-dualism is free from the intolerant moralistic heaviness that can accompany traditional religions.

But ethics has also been taught in a generous, loving, heart-centered way, even in traditional Western religions. This chapter is about heart-centered ethics. Examples are the teachings communicated by Christian gospel music and the parable of the Good Samaritan (Luke 10:25–37); by Buddhist *metta* meditations; and by the selfless service tradition of *seva* in Hinduism, in which others are seen as manifestations of divinity or global awareness and in which our actions should manifest *ahimsa* (the absence of harm). Each of these examples teaches love in an inspiring, heart-opening, non-punitive way. In fact, for the rest of this chapter, if I use the word "ethics," I'm usually referring to heart-centered ethics.

I would like to encourage those who articulate non-dual teachings, including myself, to incorporate an emphasis on heart-centered ethics.

There are many different systems of ethics. In this book, I'm not arguing for one specific ethical system among others. Rather, my point is that non-dual teachings should include *some* emphasis on ethical teachings, rather than omitting or rejecting ethics altogether.

Why Ethics?

Why am I in favor of including rather than excluding ethics? My preferences are based on my own experiences, as well as on respect for the traditional paths upon which most non-dual teachings are based. I have two fundamental reasons to prefer that ethics be a part of non-dual teachings. One is that, years before I ever encountered non-dual teachings, learning to care for others made me happier, kinder, and more peaceful. Of course, receiving heart-centered ethics teachings is no guarantee that a person will be happier or kinder. But I think the odds favor it.

The other reason that I advocate for ethics to be part of non-dual teachings is that non-dual insight seems to come a lot more readily when enabled by an open heart. The discoveries are deeper and more lasting. Heart-centered ethics teachings, when put into use, open the heart and reduce the felt insistence that everything should be about oneself. This opening assists in the exact kind of inquiry used in the direct path. I expand upon both these reasons below.

I can't lay down a prescription for a particular brand of heart-centered ethics teaching, but I can say that these teachings have helped me become happier. They have also helped me discover for myself the insights spoken of in non-dual teachings.

My Experience

I don't wish to offer my experience as something to emulate. I'm not suggesting myself as a role model. Quite the contrary. I wasn't raised with any ethical system or sensitivity to other people. There were no teachings about ethics of any type in my family. Whatever ethical sensitivities I have today were instilled by spiritual teachings. All this happened during my adult years. It's precisely because I *wasn't* raised with an ethical awareness that I've found that spiritual teachings can open the heart.

My parents were supportive in the way parenting was understood in the United States of the 1950s and 1960s. They weren't malicious or unkind. They treated us children pretty well. But we had no religion or guiding ethical view of any sort. I came to learn that there had been no religion or philosophy in my family going back at least as far as my great-grandparents' time. My parents never taught us how to be good or kind to others as a general teaching. It's not surprising that my three siblings and I have all reached out and adopted some kind of spiritual or religious teaching as adults.

Perhaps because my parents were artists, they were always more interested in their art than in other people. They were psychologically insular; they had very few friends. People rarely visited us, and my parents were never comfortable if my own friends came over to the house. Because of this, my siblings and I failed to develop the usual social skills or interpersonal sensitivities that most people grow up with. It's not that I stayed at home and had no friends. I had lots of friends and was always out and about. And I always went to very good schools. I received a great education. It's just that I had no ideas about how to treat other people. Occasionally I would witness my high-school friends operate with a degree of skill or polish in social situations. I would wonder: *How did he know to say that? To do that? It was perfect!*

For much of my life, I've been sort of oblivious to other people. In a very important way, I just didn't "see" people or their needs. They didn't register. To this day I'm much more an introvert than an extrovert.

When I was in the army (in my early twenties), my insularity acquired a sort of official doctrine. I was reading a lot of egoistic philosophy. My first inspiration was Ayn Rand and her theory of rational selfishness called "Objectivism." Later on, I progressed to something much more radical. It was a brand of hypertrophied selfishness based on the philosophy of Max Stirner. His book *The Ego and His Own: The Case of the Individual Against Authority* (Dover Publications, 2005) is an extreme example of egoism, amoralism, and irrationalism. Stirner's argument amounted to this: there's no reason for me to put any kind of normative authority above my current interests.

I developed a rebellious, argumentative, nihilistic streak. Even though I was doing my military duties at the time, I didn't accept any obligation to do so. My revolution was mostly internal. Still, that did nothing to increase my care for other people!

As a Stirnerite, I would take any opportunity to challenge proponents of ethics to answer a simple question: "Why should I be moral?" Since most of my contacts were proponents of dogmatic ethics, most of the answers boiled down to "You should because you should." Even the sociobiological approaches or answers ("It's good for the species") could never convince me. This is because they all depended upon my capitulating to something other than my current interests. All these arguments failed to move me.

In my Stirnerite way of thinking, I rejected any argument to accept authority of any kind because it asked me to put something over and above my current self. So I categorically rejected all "shoulds," including political, ethical, religious, social, contractual, and logical shoulds. No line of argument could convince me that any authority over me was justified.

I continued to feel this way for almost a decade. I even wrote graduate philosophy papers based on these ideas. And I got very good grades. But, needless to say, I wasn't becoming any more ethically sensitive to others.

Over time, I began to feel lonely and alienated. The loneliness wasn't a case of having no friends; it was a more cosmic, soulful feeling of separation. I felt cut off from what was inspiring and nourishing. I was still in graduate school and working full-time as well. One day, a Christian coworker who liked to proselytize invited me to a gospel concert. She promised that if I didn't like it, she would never bring up the subject of religion again. So I went.

I loved it! The performance was at a local church, given by a local choir personally taught by the great Edwin Hawkins of "Oh Happy Day" fame. I was deeply moved. On the surface, it was a great performance. The songs were catchy and melodic. The music had a sort of jazzy rhythm-and-blues style that appealed to me in a way that didn't require faith. And the singing was done with great heart and gusto. This was effusive gospel music of the Pentecostal type. I was clapping and swaying back and forth with the rest of the audience. But something more profound was happening too. I felt a kind of opening. I felt as if a kind of light was addressing the dark loneliness that had been creeping up on me for several years.

The next day at work, I unashamedly asked my coworker to suggest more of these events. Over the next few weeks, she kept me well informed of upcoming musical performances, all the while with a kindly and understanding gleam in her eye.

One evening at a gospel concert, I felt an earth-shattering change come over me. I felt shivers run up and down my spine. A sizzle erupted out of the top of my head and shot down the backs of my legs. Afterward, I felt like orienting myself more toward this light. Quite suddenly, even as a movie buff, I lost interest in horror movies. I stopped cursing, a habit I'd picked up in the army. I listened to more gospel music. I felt a yearning to be around its message.

Nobody was telling me to do this. I totally lost interest in Max Stirner's teachings. I joined a church very much like the one where I had attended that first concert.

For the first time in my life, starting in 1986, I began to value other people. In the church, I encountered a Christian vocabulary and a Christian set of teachings for all the experiences I was having. And as an active member of the church, I encountered ethical teachings. Looking back now, I would designate those teachings as the heart-centered ethics type, not the dogmatic ethics type.

Of course the Christian system can exemplify dogmatic ethics in an abusive way. But it's also rich enough to have room for the heart-centered kind as well. Christianity engages heart-centered ethics in a way that encompasses thought, speech, and action. In Christianity, you learn through "precept and example," which basically means theory, practice, and emulation. You learn specific ways of treating others, many of which are codified in rules. The rules in the Pentecostal Christian church to which I belonged in the late 1980s included the necessity of going to church at least several times a week; serving and giving generously to others; turning the other cheek when someone does or says something hurtful; refraining from lying, cheating, and stealing from others; and refraining from any kind of sex (even kissing) before marriage or outside of marriage.

This was all new to me. My parents had never covered anything like this. I began to comply with the rules and recommendations as best I could. It's not that I started to believe that these particular rules were the best of all possible rules or that God preferred them to all others. What happened to me wasn't a matter of belief. It was more an inclination of the heart. This was a kind of development I'd never encountered before.

I began to see that the specific heartfelt ethical teachings, even the rules, had their place. Even though my change of heart at the gospel concert had given me a spontaneous yearning to do good, it had given me no concrete ways of putting it into practice. I had no idea of what to do in specific life situations. The bright and open benevolence I began to feel after the concert wasn't enough in and of itself to bring my behavior in line with the Christian view of life. In other words, for me to behave respectfully and graciously toward others and toward God, as directed by Christianity, I needed specific ethical teachings. These teachings became very much a part of my entire Christian experience. I noticed that the heart-centered ethics teachings I learned in church (in combination with the transformational experience itself) made me feel happier and more closely connected to other people than I had ever felt in my life. Since that time, I've never felt lonely or alienated again.

After graduate school, I found employment in another city. My commitment to Pentecostal Christianity turned into a broader spiritual search. In the church, I had not integrated my thinking mind with my heart-centered spiritual experiences, and I felt an urge to do so. So after I moved, I became an avid spiritual explorer.

I looked into many paths. Several paths—among them Rosicrucianism, Zen Buddhism, traditional Advaita Vedanta, Pure Land, and Madhyamika Buddhism—included robust heart-centered ethics components. And several paths—among them the teachings of Ramesh Balsekar and the direct path of Shri Atmananda—had no official ethical component to speak of.

Among the paths that included heart-centered ethics teachings, I saw that the lessons I had learned in Christianity about the importance of ethics were confirmed. Not that I found other systems to agree perfectly with Christianity on what they recommended or prohibited; rather, I found that other paths regarded heart-centered ethics as an essential part of the package. I found that when I followed the heart-centered ethical recommendations, I experienced a more open heart and a greater overall feeling of happiness. And it occurred to me, based on my experience in various spiritual paths, that paths actually need some sort of heart-centered ethical teaching. I felt that paths need ethics to help with two related goals that paths usually have. One goal is to articulate a vision for how life should be lived. The other goal is to inspire students to work toward that vision. Even if the vision is something vague like "live in a free, enlightened way," I thought my chances of freedom and enlightenment would be much better if the path also had an ethical component.

It seemed that the ethical components of these paths weren't a side issue. The ethical component seemed intrinsically necessary to each path's spiritual goals.

Here are some specific examples of the spiritual benefits of ethical teachings. In my time with various Rosicrucian groups, I noticed an emphasis on loving one's neighbor. In the Zen temple I attended most frequently, there was a lot of emphasis on compassion and deferring to others. Compassion and deference were enacted in many concrete ways. In the traditional Advaita Vedanta school where I took weekly classes for several years, there was an emphasis on treating all beings as manifestations of the highest deity. Sometimes the teachings would advise us to treat all women as we would treat our own mother and to treat all men as we would treat our own father. In Tibetan Madhyamika Buddhism, I noticed a constant emphasis on putting compassion (defined as the altruistic aspiration to achieve the highest enlightenment for the sake of all beings) into practice by making vows and by developing generosity, discipline, patience, perseverance, meditative concentration, and wisdom. Thanks to the heart-centered ethics component of each of these paths, my self-concern softened; I adopted a more engaged, concrete, benevolent way of interacting with people; and I experienced a warm, expansive joy. I only hope that, as a result of these changes in me, people found me more pleasant to be around!

Ethics as Preparation for Non-dual Realization

Both Advaita Vedanta and Madhyamika Buddhism teach that cultivating an ethical outlook in life is preparation for the deep insights required for what they consider non-dual realization. These paths also define realization in a holistic way that incorporates an ethical orientation toward others. According to these paths, if a person has had deep insights and yet treats others poorly, that person hasn't yet reached the highest possible realization. Both of these paths are heavy with formal inquiry (called jnana yoga in Vedanta and "emptiness meditation" in Madhyamika). Both of these paths teach a form of heart-centered ethics and relate it intimately with inquiry. There are traces of this ethical approach in the direct path as well.

As these paths see it, an ethical orientation is needed for two reasons. First, living life in accordance with ethics makes life more pleasant for everyone. As I mentioned above, my experience agrees with this reason to embrace ethics.

The other reason is spiritually pragmatic and bears more directly on inquiry: living life in accordance with ethics prepares the mind to be more open and subtle. This openness helps enable the deep insights required for non-dual insight. There's even what one might call an official ethical gatekeeping moment, in which students are urged to internalize the ethical teachings before proceeding with the radical, penetrating non-dual investigations. In a manner of speaking, ethics are a prerequisite to the highest forms of realization these paths teach.

Traditional Advaita Vedanta

Advaita Vedanta speaks of prerequisites as qualifications for one's suitability to study Vedanta. Adi Shankaracharya's *Tattva Bodha* lays out what are called the *Sadhana Chatushtaya*, or fourfold qualifications, to be a suitable student of Advaita Vedanta.[8] The four qualifications (which involve ethics as well as character traits) are as follows:

1. **Discrimination** (*viveka*)—the capacity to tell apart the real and the unreal, or the permanent (Brahman, awareness) and the impermanent (everything else)

2. **Dispassion** (*vairagya*)—detachment or the absence of desire for the enjoyment of sense objects

3. **The six behavioral traits** (*shamadi shatka sampatti*)—the fruits of spiritual practice, described below:

- Control of the mind (*shama*)—an attitude of tranquility and contentment, in which the mind doesn't get caught up in the signals of the senses

- Cultivation of the senses (*dama*)—an ability to keep the body free from getting involved in what the senses may find appealing (This amounts to using your senses and body for the good of others and for your own spiritual development.)

- Withdrawal (*uparati*)—a condition of the mind in which the mind isn't influenced by sensory objects (This is achieved through wisdom, in which you realize that sensory objects can't bring about lasting happiness.)

- Forbearance (*titiksha*)—the ability to endure sorrowful states and events without anxiety, resentment, or indignation

- Faith (*shraddha*)—unwavering conviction about the elements of the path, including the scriptures, the ethical guidelines they contain, the teacher, and the self

- Concentration (*samadhana*)—the ability to focus benevolently and single-pointedly, especially on the Absolute

4. **Desire for freedom** (*mumukshutva*)—desire for self-knowledge, in order to be liberated from the bondage that comes from identification with the body and mind (This is not a desire for any kind of spiritual status or acclaim, but rather a sincere and intense desire for freedom.)

How are ethics involved in all of this? These four qualifications aren't ethical statements, but ethics become involved when you carry out the actual practices of which these are the fruits.

Here's an example from my own life. Before I encountered the direct path, I studied Advaita Vedanta for several years with the Chinmaya Mission. This prominent school of traditional Advaita Vedanta, with teaching centers in India, the United States, and Canada, emphasizes ethics very strongly. Ethics are taught as important for living in society and as an essential precursor to the difficult subtleties of self-inquiry.

Our small class comprised mostly Western students. As such, we weren't asked to perform many specifically Hindu spiritual practices. But we were encouraged to respect ahimsa (non-harming) and to do karma yoga and bhakti yoga every day to benefit our character in general, as well as to reduce our egocentrism and self-concern.

Karma yoga was explained as service to others in which, instead of expecting personal reward, we would dedicate the fruits of our actions to Brahman (or our chosen deity) or to the good of all. We were told the service must be sincerely other-directed—we were encouraged not to perform karma yoga for the express purpose of preparing ourselves for liberation, because that kind of motivation subtly reasserts egocentric concerns. As I practiced karma yoga, I noticed that my mind became more able to function without needing to catalog the benefits accruing to me. This opened my mind and my heart, and it helped with my contemplative self-inquiry when it got subtle or abstract.

Bhakti yoga was explained as devotion to the self (Brahman, awareness). Our teacher pointed out that it would be easier to focus our devotion if, for each of us, the self had some sort of phenomenal representation. Toward this end, our teacher recommended that we take up one of the Hindu deities, such as Krishna, Shiva, Shakti, Vishnu, or Brahma. The Hindu deities have different aspects, personalities, and abilities, and we were encouraged to review the various deities with an eye to how they could assist in our Vedantic study. Our teacher was particularly fond of Durga, who's frequently depicted as an eight-armed female warrior. Durga's ability to assist in Vedantic study is due to her destroyer character. She destroys the ignorance that prevents us from knowing our true nature.

I felt a natural attraction to Durga's powerful goddess aspect, which reminded me of La Virgen de Guadalupe, the Black Madonna, and Kwan Yin. So I set up an altar with her image. I meditated on her image and prayed to her to destroy ignorance. I felt sweetness and an expansion of my heart and goodwill. What was important for me was that I was devoting my energies not toward a particular image or entity but toward a symbol of everything. Durga's symbolic nature was able to universalize my devotional energies, carrying them beyond the image itself. This had ethical consequences. In doing my daily devotions, I felt a sweet, oceanic broadening of loving feelings, which remained with me for hours. It grew into a constant sense of benevolence. I felt I could understand in an intuitive way the Vedantic ethical guideline to treat all beings as manifestations of the Absolute.

The ethical teachings in traditional Advaita Vedanta, at least in my own urbanized Western experience of it, were a good example of heart-centered ethics rather than dogmatic ethics. There was no uncompromising set of rules that we were threatened with. Instead, the teachings were given in a kindhearted way, in which we students sincerely felt that the teacher and the teachings supported our spiritual quest. I felt the effects of these ethical teachings in my daily life. My thoughts, speech, and actions became more observant and caring of others. I also noticed how I was able to remain steadier with self-inquiry.

Madhyamika Buddhism

Madhyamika, like traditional Advaita Vedanta, is a spiritual path in which analysis and inquiry are prominent. It also emphasizes ethical teachings as essential to realization. In Madhyamika, students are encouraged to develop deep compassion (*karuna*) as a prerequisite to being taught emptiness. The dialogue at the beginning of this chapter is a dramatization of this point. When meditating on compassion, followers of Madhyamika develop the sincere wish that others be happy and free of suffering. When meditating on emptiness, they meditate on how the self, other beings, and the world don't exist in the substantial, exaggerated way we usually imagine. Emptiness and compassion are often described as two sides of the same coin.

Personally, compassion helps my meditation on emptiness in this way: it strengthens my motivation. This is a familiar phenomenon even in the everyday sense. If you're a working person, you'll have more motivation to continue on the job through tough times if you have a family depending on you. When emptiness meditations get tough, you'll do a better job of sticking to them if you feel that they'll benefit not just you but also other beings.[9] And emptiness meditations can definitely get tough, because you'll discover that you don't exist in the inherent way you had imagined.

Practicing compassion helps me in another way as well. It fills my heart with love. It opens my heart, allowing my self-concern to diminish. In *The Art of Happiness in a Troubled World*, the Dalai Lama is quoted as saying, "If you want others to be happy, practice compassion. If you want to be happy, practice compassion."[10]

When I practice compassion, my mind feels clearer and is less demanding that inquiry satisfy the current needs of my separate self. I become more insightful, more subtle, and more able to realize emptiness.

Indeed, my own experience with this path agrees with its teachings—it's much easier for me to realize emptiness when I approach the meditations with a compassionate heart.

Ethics and Realization

These two formal paths—Advaita Vedanta and Madhyamika—agree about the importance of an ethical outlook. When I internalize the heart-centered ethics teachings, I see beneficial effects for others and myself. One of the benefits is that the paths' own spiritual goals seem easier for me to reach.

Do ethics still matter once you've reached these goals? The two paths have different rhetorical descriptions of realization. They don't leave it up to the power of realization to impart ethical thought, speech, and action. I look at the relationship between ethics and realization in these paths in the following way. As a student of the path, you're taught a sense of ethics and the recommended ways of interacting with people (and non-human entities). These teachings are part of your spiritual training, and they help you become a more loving, considerate person. Not only does your realization depend on this ethical orientation, your realization isn't expected to cause a drastic change in how you treat other beings.

What I find significant for non-dualism is the fact that both of these powerful paths teach ethics in the first place. Neither path expects ethical conduct to proceed merely from realization itself. I consider this an important point for non-dualism, and I'll return to it shortly.

Against Ethics in Non-dualism

My personal experience is that ethics are essential in non-dual teachings. But not everyone feels this way. There are several popular critiques according to which ethics should definitely *not* be part of non-dual teachings. You may have encountered versions of these critiques in your exploration of non-dual teachings. In what follows, I discuss three types of critiques and the reasons why they fail.

Critique 1: Ethics are counterproductive. This is the critique I've mentioned several times already. According to this critique, non-dual teachings should be descriptive, not prescriptive. Any kind of ethics would be a prescriptive teaching, which is a teaching that posits what we should, in some sense, do. Any prescriptive teaching can only address a so-called person. A person is not the self of awareness, but only an arising that appears to awareness. Such a teaching can't apply to the Ultimate, which is our true nature. If a non-dual teaching keeps telling us that we should do one thing and not another, we'll only feel more separate than we already do.

Actually, I understand this critique quite well, because I used to feel similarly about prescriptive claims of any kind. During my younger, rebellious Stirnerite phase, when people told me what I should do, it made me feel aggressive and argumentative. Looking back now, I see that I was largely objecting to ethical teachings of the dogmatic kind. Ethics taught this way tell you what you're supposed to do and take the position that you're already obligated, whether you agree or not. Or such ethics may threaten you with misfortune.

It seems to me that critique 1 applies only to dogmatic ethics teachings and not heart-centered ethics teachings. In my opinion, it's the dogmatic, fear-inducing ethics teachings that give the whole subject a bad name. These ethics actually *contribute* to entification, the feeling of being a strongly defined and separate being. When being ethically berated in an unloving, threatening way, a person is being addressed verbally and physically as if his or her true identity is a person trapped in a body.

I can understand why people who had suffered under a system of dogmatic ethics would find relief in non-dual teachings that promise ultimate freedom without mentioning ethics.

But again, this entire critique applies only to the dogmatic approach. It fails to show why heart-centered ethics shouldn't be part of non-dual teachings. My own experience with heart-centered ethics teachings has been extremely positive. Having experienced various kinds of heart-centered ethics teachings for myself, I've never found them to contribute to a sense of separation. They've had the opposite effect, actually, contributing to a greater feeling of freedom and connection with others.

Critique 2: Ethics are false or irrelevant. The key phrase in this critique is that "the sage is not involved." Here's a supporting passage from a book called *Awakening to Consciousness*. (I apologize for the length, but the passage deserves to appear in its entirety.)

Having totally accepted that the Source is the only doer, the Sage is constantly at peace, but equally, he is just like any ordinary person, a bodymind—computer programmed by Source registered as destiny in his genes. Therefore, the genes in a Sage may bring about an action, which could even be condemned by the society or even by the law of the Country. So, the Sage's actions may result in some recognition from society, but also condemnation, yet the Sage is not involved in the results, as he knows he is not the doer: sometimes there may arise a sense of pleasure, a sense of regret, but never pride and arrogance, guilt and shame. The Sage does not even react if an action of his is condemned. The Sage accepts it with a sense of regret, but as it has happened, the Sage has to accept the result of that condemned action.[11]

According to this critique, non-dualism shouldn't include an ethics component because there's nothing for ethics to apply to in the first place. Actions that look like helping or harming may emanate from the "Sage," or they may not. Whatever happens isn't due to personal agency. There's no personal agency anywhere. Still, having deep insight won't change your behavior and turn you into a murderer or a bank robber. Thus, the teaching of even heart-centered ethics would be, at best, irrelevant.

One problem with the quoted passage is that the discussion of the non-existence of doership is entirely in terms of the sage. How can the sage be the only one for whom the Source is the doer? Of course the sage is defined here as one who has accepted that there's no personal doership. But actually, according to this teaching, there's no doer anywhere. The lack of doership itself should apply to everyone, not just the sage. Why is the position of "not involved" only for the sage? For example, in my amoralist, nihilist Stirnerite way of thinking, there was no conception of a "Sage." The insight that nothing was to be placed above personal interests was for anyone and everyone. Under the influence of Stirnerism, I was unkind to many people. I was also "not involved" because I found ethics to be limiting and irrelevant. I hurt many people by being an argumentative jerk. Feeling an aggressive, arrogant, superior glee, I would start arguments and end up being insensitive and verbally hurtful. And I never felt bothered by the consequences. I was having fun! Was I covered by the "not involved" principle? Yes, because it applies to everyone. The "not involved" principle applies to amoralists and nihilists too. This doesn't make critique 2 very appealing!

Critique 2 is partial and privileges the sage, when by rights it applies to everyone, since everyone lacks personal agency just as the sage does. This partiality leads us to the second point: this critique functions to spiritually legitimize objectionable behavior on the part of those who consider themselves enlightened.

We usually hear the anti-ethical teaching that "the sage is not involved" at precisely those times when the sage has been performing some action that others have reported is painful or harmful.[12] Why is it mostly *then* that these ethical pronouncements about the sage are heard? This seems very convenient for the sage. The convenience seems like what Western logicians call the fallacy of special pleading, a kind of psychological fallacy, which applies a principle in an uneven way. This double standard serves to rationalize an action and benefit a particular, preselected person. Personally, I find critique 2 and its anti-ethical approach logically suspicious, psychologically unbalanced, and spiritually unhelpful.

In addition, this critique seems to be falling out of favor. These days, more and more people expect some kind of ethical accountability in the area of non-dual teachings. People find the idea of a sage who can abuse others and still be granted the status of sage to be abhorrent. This might not have been the case back in the 1990s, when non-dual teachings were new and it seemed that non-duality could do no wrong. But I think that many people involved in non-dual teachings just don't find critiques like this one to be convincing anymore.

Critique 3: Ethics are unnecessary. Whereas critique 2 asserts that the sage is not involved in ethical or unethical behavior, this critique asserts that the sage always behaves ethically. It asserts that by virtue of being a sage, the enlightened one always acts in a loving, compassionate way that benefits all. Therefore, we don't need to include ethics in non-dual teachings. The very event of enlightenment takes care of everything.

I've heard this critique delivered in two different styles. One style sounds similar to critique 2 in its defensive, rationalizing tone. It states that ethical teachings are unnecessary in a non-dual path because when a person becomes enlightened, he or she will automatically act for the good of all concerned. A proponent of this view might argue: "I realize that I'm Love, Knowledge, and Being. I no longer act from the perspective of a person; I act from the universal. As an enlightened one, I no longer have a sense of separation. Ethics can't apply to me. All actions flowing through 'this' mind-body mechanism issue directly from the Love that is my nature. As unconditioned Love, I am the Absolute. The Absolute isn't unethical, so how can any actions that flow from the Absolute be unethical?"

If I lend my ear to this presentation of critique 3, listening not for truth so much as tone, it sounds hyped and overblown. I've heard too many guru scandals rationalized by these elevated and self-privileging terms.

The high-toned, worshipful language sounds as if it's trying to pull a fast one. The language has the beseeching, manipulative tone of an advertisement. Unconditional love is a quality of openness that applies to the Source, as awareness. But I feel as though I'm being asked to make a perspective shift in which I attribute this loving unconditionality to a finite, particular person who seeks to be treated in an exalted way. I feel as if I'm being asked to buy into something. I almost want to tap my pocket to make sure my wallet is still there. This critique is worded in a style that simply won't be convincing to contemporary observers of the non-dual scene. Indeed, critiques like this one seem to be less common these days than, say, fifteen years ago.

But this critique can be stated in a more sensible way, as I examine next.

Critique 3R (revised): Ethical teachings aren't needed because, having realized one's true nature, one will inevitably and spontaneously act in the best interest of all beings concerned in the situation. This is a much more reasonable statement of critique 3. The crux of its meaning is that something important happens when people realize their true nature, and it has a positive effect on their behavior.

I agree about the positive effect on behavior. But I don't agree that ethical teachings aren't needed. Even though something fundamentally important happens when people realize their true nature, it still isn't sufficient to guarantee that they'll always act in the best interest of all beings concerned in the situation. In what follows, I say more about why I think ethical teachings are needed.

But first, what happens when people realize their true nature? In terms of the direct path, they realize that they're not a person, a mind, or a body. They realize that they're nothing other than awareness, which is the nature of all.

In an important sense, this realization isn't personal. If I (Greg) have realized my true nature, it's not only Greg who's not a person or an agent of actions. There are no true persons, agents, or actions anywhere. All these things are nothing more than arisings—which is to say, nothing other than awareness. And if the transparent witness has collapsed (see chapter 9), then I can't even seriously claim that there are arisings. Because no dualities are experienced, it doesn't seem that anything appears, disappears, arises, or falls. Even talking about it is a nonreferential affair, more akin to poetry than science.

Greg gets out of the way. "Greg," which used to be the central focus of actions as well as their supposed point of origin, is realized to be neither. There's no reason to privilege Greg over anything else. There's nothing that has any obligation to Greg. Greg is no different from a puff of smoke.

In the spirit of joyful irony, I can say that the effect on my behavior is through my mind and my heart. Even my body is reoriented.

So then what happens? I feel a vast love for everything and all beings. I feel an overwhelming love that reaches out to find ways of helping. I don't feel a desire to harm others. Even more, I feel motivated to help promote welfare to the extent I can. I can't find any other important reason to do anything. I can help in little ways, such as by smiling at someone on the street. And I may be called upon to help in a big way, such as by laying my life down for someone. I don't know, and I'm not sure what'll happen.

It's this overwhelming love that brings me to my disagreement with critique 3R. According to critique 3R, after having realized my true nature, *I will inevitably and spontaneously act in the best interest of all beings concerned in the situation.* This places the entire burden of effective ethical action upon insight alone, leaving out many other critical factors.

Critique 3R claims that insight is enough. I disagree. Whatever it takes to act in the best interest of all beings concerned in the situation requires more than mere non-dual insight. I vote to add some kind of ethical teachings to the package. Even then, there's no guarantee that effective ethical action will take place. But I think that ethical teachings make ethical action more likely. Insight, together with an ethical orientation, will equip people in mind and body with a powerful set of ways and means of treating one another more kindly.

Every once in a while, I hear stories about an enlightened person who does amazingly right and relevant things. All these "enlightened actions" are attributed solely to the person's awakening, with no credit to the ethical and cultural education the person may have received. Why discount those formative aspects?

So Why Isn't Insight Enough?

Non-dual realization is helpful, for sure. People who are enlightened will act without calculation and without egocentric expectations that their actions must benefit themselves. But more specificity is needed. Some kind of ethical pointers or guidelines are needed, because insight is too vague for the complexity of specific situations we encounter in life. As I discussed earlier, my own ethical education has been desultory. My parents never delivered ethical teachings to the family, and I didn't grow up in a religious, spiritual, or heart-centered way. So I know what it's like in practice to have no idea what to do in an ethical sense, even if I have good intentions. I know what it's like not to have been equipped with the usual tools for helping people effectively. I didn't spend my formative years undergoing the depth of training that produces the kind of spontaneous responses considered to constitute ethical action. Because of these aspects of my upbringing, and because I was an amoralist and a nihilist, I'm in favor of at least some amount of ethical teaching in non-dualism or any other spiritual endeavor.

This applies to the time after non-dual insight as well. In my case, my heart and mind were open and loving, but I didn't have what musicians call "chops." To some extent, an ethical orientation is dispositional: people build up compassionate "reflexes" through habitual compassionate action. These prepare them for spontaneous action when things are happening too fast for their mind to process. We could look at effective ethical action as being dependent on certain skills.[13]

For example, many skills are associated with an altruistic and beneficial orientation toward others. There are active skills, such as being able to perform CPR, execute the Heimlich maneuver, or save a person from drowning. These skills can also include speech and action. For example, my family never attended funerals. When I finally attended my first funeral as an adult, I became acutely aware of not knowing what to say. For this reason, I can imagine that at a funeral, rather than "I'm sorry," "My sympathy to your family," "If you ever wish to talk, I'm just a phone call away," or "You and your loved one will be in my thoughts," someone who had received no practical ethical education might very well say something correct in terms of non-dual insight but incredibly insensitive, such as "There are no persons. A person is merely an arising in awareness."

My point is not that we all have an obligation to rush out and learn these things but rather that these kinds of effective actions are types of skills. They contribute to what we think of as "in the best interest of all beings concerned in the situation" that critique 3R asserts. And being able to perform these actions at the right time is a matter of learning and cultivation, not simply a matter of non-dual insight. By critique 3R's own definition, some kind of ethical education seems necessary.

In Favor of Ethical Teachings—Example

Here's a simple but important example from my own life. It's an example of how non-dual insight by itself isn't enough to produce action that benefits all concerned. In my example, non-dual insight was assisted by something from the local context. In this case, it was a simple word. One small word served to add direction to the general openness that came from insight. That word made all the difference.

Several decades ago, while in the early stages of my non-dual inquiry, I was a freelance writer doing movie and book reviews. One week, I had the idea to write a review of a transgender (male-to-female) beauty pageant being held at a New York City bar. It would feature the usual pageant categories, including sportswear, swimwear, evening gown, and talent.

Before the event, I interviewed the bar owner. She told me that New York had a large community of male-to-female performers, dancers, singers, lip-synchers and celebrity impersonators. Some of them had undergone quite a bit of surgery. Others relied on natural looks, clothing, and makeup. Regardless, every participant had joined this event to celebrate the expression of femininity. I was fascinated and told the owner that I would like to interview some of the contestants.

At first the owner was skeptical of my intentions. Journalists had done write-ups before, and they had only poked fun at the whole scene. I replied that I was sincerely interested. I wanted to do a sympathetic review, and I promised to let her see a copy before I sent it to the editors. She said okay, and we began to walk backstage to meet some of the performers. On the way, I asked her,

"How do I refer to them? As 'he' or 'she'?"

"Whoever you talk to," she said, "treat her like a lady."

"Lady." "She." Small words. But I took them deeply to heart and sincerely honored them. In a harmonious way, these words reoriented my approach to the people I met. I wrote the article, everyone at the bar loved it, and I became good friends with the owner, the members of staff, and many of the ladies. I learned that they saw themselves as ladies in wonderfully nuanced, creative, and inspirational ways. I learned about the importance and sensitivity of language in their social context. I learned that in their particular milieu, the appearance of gender is a matter of art and heart. The linguistic and gender issues assume paramount importance. If I had used the wrongly gendered word even innocently, I would've been invalidating the femininity they expressed so well.

I'll always appreciate that small lesson from the bar owner. Looking back, I notice that in my original question to her, I was of course saying (and thinking) "he" first. To this day, I consider her response a simple but profound heart-centered ethics teaching that I needed in that context. I had some degree of non-dual insight (perhaps enough to ask her the question?), but to this day I don't see how insight alone would've prevented me from causing others heartache and pain by using the wrong word. I needed the ethics teaching.

To summarize this objection to critique 3R, even though the critique sounds reasonable and impressive, it's false in my experience. Some ethical teaching is needed.

There's another reason not to accept critique 3R. What about all those people who haven't yet realized the truth of their nature? Even if 3R were accurate about what happens upon realization, it would leave everyone else without any ethical teaching until they come to the end. Why wait?

Finally, I would like to revisit a point I made earlier in this chapter. Traditional Advaita Vedanta and Madhyamika Buddhism, which rely heavily on inquiry to foster the discovery of truth, don't accept critique 3R or any of the other critiques of ethics I discuss. They teach ethics and don't minimize or omit the importance of ethics. According to these paths, the ethical orientation you have before insight will continue after insight. As your realization deepens, your understanding will deepen. Your creativity and spontaneity will deepen as well. But in no case do these traditions place the burden of effective ethical action on insight alone.

I find it interesting that Shri Atmananda, who doesn't really mention ethics very much, nevertheless honors the possibility that ethical teaching can be a profound route to self-knowledge. Here's one of the fuller examples he gives, in which he visualizes the Hindu Brahman marriage as an example of selfless love helping carry a couple to the Ultimate.

> In married life they cultivate the art of selfless love, each sacrificing the interest of the lower [personal] self for the sake of the partner. Ultimately, they come to understand that each of them does not love the other for the sake of the other, but for the sake of the self in the other—the self which is indivisible and one.
>
> Thus they are enabled to reach the ultimate Truth by following the ideal married life, of course after initiation by a Karana-guru, without the need of any other *sadhana*.[14]

The idea of selfless love assisting our understanding seems a very fruitful approach for a non-dual path. It would be helpful to incorporate teachings like this into non-dualism.

So, What Kind of Ethics?

This is where I have no specific proposals. The type of ethics one adopts is an individual matter. People who are interested in non-dual teachings come from vastly different backgrounds and have different resonances. It makes no sense to prescribe one ethical teaching across the board. Instead, as stated at the beginning of this chapter, the main point I wish to make here is that non-dual teachings should give at least some importance to ethics. The effects of the non-dual portion of a person's spiritual teaching would be not to refute ethics or make ethics into ironclad rules but to transform ethics by integrating them with the path's wisdom.

So my plea to others would merely be "Please, think about incorporating at least some kind of ethical considerations into how you engage and communicate spirituality."

As for me, I've been doing several things along these lines, and I'll probably do more in the future. I emphasize how ethics have been helpful in my journey. Also, when I discuss spiritual topics with people, I follow a code of ethics from the American Philosophical Practitioners Association.[15] I endeavor to

- do no harm;

- respect the welfare, integrity, dignity, autonomy, and privacy of others;

- be sensitive to alternative worldviews and philosophical perspectives;

- avoid creating dependency on me;

- avoid sexual intimacy or any other form of dual role that would compromise the integrity of the communicative relationship;

- promote mutual understanding, cooperation, and respect between my own modality and others; and

- promote ethical practice.

I don't try to personalize the teachings or make them about *me*. I like to keep things down-to-earth. I don't offer myself as someone to emulate. My style is more like that of a college professor or jovial uncle. When I work with groups of people, I much prefer the university seminar format to the *satsang* format. I feel that the seminar format exhibits a less dramatic power differential between teacher and students. In seminars, everyone sits around a table. The focus of attention shifts from person to person; it doesn't stay locked on one privileged speaker. The seminar format is more like a dialogue or polylogue and less like a speech or monologue. This doesn't mean that it isn't experiential or that we can't work with the body. All this is included.

There are some teaching archetypes that aren't my style, such as fool, clown, jester, Zen master, trickster, and disapproving nun. As styles, I like them all, but I'm not wired to use any of them. I'm also content not to use the famous "crazy wisdom" style. Crazy wisdom teachings can seem like a paradox or even a negation of ethics—I'm not exactly sure. But I know that many times when I've had discussions about the importance of ethics, people cite crazy wisdom as a way to negate the importance of ethics. They narrate examples of famous teachers doing something that onlookers considered unethical or even harmful to the student. According to the narratives, the teacher's actions derived from a higher wisdom unavailable to onlookers and even to us as consumers of the narrative. The actions were supposed to benefit the student and to facilitate radical breakthroughs. But of course crazy wisdom has also served as a defense for selfish and harmful behavior on the part of the teacher. I feel fine not utilizing this method, even if it limits my options for helping others.

Transparency

I honor the thinking behind the call for teachers to be transparent about what they're doing. Transparency is a relatively new idea in non-dualism. I have a feeling that the specific implications of transparency for non-dual communication are still a work in progress. For example, how do we balance the call for transparency with respect for privacy?

Oftentimes the call for transparency in the non-dual context involves money. Indeed, *Merriam-Webster's* dictionary even includes a definition of "transparent" that bears on money: characterized by visibility or accessibility of information especially concerning business practices (*Merriam Webster*, 11th ed., s.v. "transparent"). Is it ethical to charge for non-dual teachings? And if so, what would transparency have us report about it?

About a decade ago, there was a two-year period when I charged a sliding-scale hourly consulting fee, under the auspices of a philosophical consulting relationship, to talk about non-dual teachings. In Western culture, philosophical consulting is an ancient profession that received a new lease on life with the 1999 publication of Lou Marinoff's *Plato, Not Prozac! Applying Eternal Wisdom to Everyday Problems*.[16] I took a training workshop in Italy with Professor Marinoff, which, along with my formal education, qualified me for certification from the American Philosophical Practitioners Association. I continue to work with Professor Marinoff on the scholarly journal entitled *Philosophical Practice*. There are many types of philosophical consulting, depending on the interests of the client. The issues can be ethical dilemmas, life choices, existential questions, or issues of organizational goals.

So I created a website and began a small part-time business. I worked closely with people one-on-one, spending many hours together on the phone and in person. In the classic Hippocratic way, if I ever thought that the client could receive more effective help from another modality, such as medicine, dentistry, psychotherapy, financial accounting, or a philosophical area that I wasn't familiar with, I would refer him or her to another practitioner right away.

Over time, it turned out that most of the reporting issues weren't the classic philosophical problems that my fellow philosophical practitioners were getting. Instead, they were requests for help with non-dual inquiry. When this really dawned on me, I thought about the fact that all the most significant non-dual teachings I ever received came from written material, free classes, and the most casual one-on-one conversations. How could I charge others for what I had gotten for free? The very idea of charging became intolerable to me. Besides, I love talking about these things. It's never a "job." To this day, I follow the American Philosophical Practitioners Association's code of ethics and help with its scholarly journal, but I no longer charge money to speak with people about these issues.

Where to Go from Here?

Again, I'm not sure about specifics. Myself, I'll be looking for more ways to incorporate ethics into non-dual teaching. One thing I *cannot* recommend is a standard program or universal set of ethical guidelines for everyone to adopt. That would make no sense, given human diversity. And of course it has the makings of the dogmatic, totalitarian type of ethics teaching that people rightly reject.

When I think about the heart-opening ethics teachings that I've received, both inside and outside of "official" non-dual teaching contexts, I'm filled with tears of joy. And awe. These teachings have made me happier in countless ways and improved my interpersonal relationships. And I still consider myself a beginner! I consider heart-centered ethics teachings to be crucial for non-dual inquiry. In my experience, these teachings have been indispensable preparation for the mental, physical, and energetic shifts involved in non-dual insight. I can't recommend these teachings highly enough!

CHAPTER 3

The Language of Joyful Irony

Dear Greg,

This is the body-mind mechanism known as Jason Andrews,[17] who has written before. There has been the experience of no-self happening here. First there is the experience, but then it is gone. Can it be stable?

This organism will be in the New York City area this coming April. Would it be possible for this apparatus and that one to get together for a cup of coffee sometime? It is known that there is no time or space, and objects are just consciousness, but words must be used.

Sincerely, Jason.

In this chapter, I'd like to discuss the approach to language used in the direct path. I call this approach "nonreferential." Simply put, nonreferentiality is an approach to language that doesn't assume the existence of subjects or objects. Thinking in a nonreferential way about language can be a very freeing complement to self-inquiry.[18]

In the direct path, nonreferentiality results from seeing through the myth of objective existence. It supports the insights and direct seeings that happen in your inquiry. And if inquiry isn't your strength, you can set it aside and engage nonreferentiality directly through language, poetry, music, and song. You can even look at vision, sense of hearing, and sense of touch as languages. One thing I like about nonreferentiality is that it yields a greater freedom of expression than our regular attitude toward language. It's also a natural component of joyful irony, which I discuss later in this chapter and in chapter 10, "After Awareness: The End of the Path."

The "Realist" View of Language— Representationalism

The nonreferential approach is very different from our usual way of thinking about language. Usually we feel sure that nouns refer to existing objects. We think that pronouns such as "I," "you," and "she" refer to existing people. And we think that sentences refer to existing facts. When someone is speaking, we sometimes get the feeling that there must be something out there for the words to refer to. Why else would there be a word for it?

Let's call this the "representationalist" approach to language. Representationalism usually assumes some kind of relationship between words and their referents. It may be that objects *cause* our words through a complex chain of events. Or that words are *mental pictures* of objects or *point* to objects. Of course non-dual teachings don't have us think about these linguistic issues too much. They try to have us get behind or beyond language. But Shri Atmananda talks about language more than many other teachers do. He provides the seeds of a helpful and freeing way to think about language. I explore more of this below.

The message from Jason above was an e-mail I received that shows how even exponents of non-dual teachings can be seduced by the representationalist approach to language. The circumlocutions in Jason's e-mail are obvious. Plus, they make his message harder to understand. Let's take a look at a few of them:

Avoidance of pronouns: "the body-mind mechanism," "here," "this apparatus"

Non-dual disclaimers: "there is no time or space," "objects are just consciousness"

Strained passive voice: "There has been the experience…" "It is known that…"

Apology for the unavoidable: "…but words must be used"

(By the way, when Jason and I met up, we went for pizza and had a great conversation. After we sat down and ordered, he apologized again for using words. But after that, the conversation was quite normal!)

So why would someone feel the need to communicate like this? I'm sure that Jason wanted me to know that he didn't think he existed as a truly existent entity. I got that. I interpreted the circumlocutions as a kind of non-dual greeting card. But also, I got the sense that Jason was trying to be *accurate*. He was exercising care not to use a word to refer to something that didn't exist. So Jason didn't want to use the words "I" and "you," because he was sure that the personal *I* and the personal *you* were imaginary entities that didn't exist. He was also apologetic about referring to a month and a place to meet for coffee, because there isn't anything that truly bears these labels. But since it's hard to suggest a meeting in any other way, he used the terms and then apologized for using them.

In other words, Jason still subscribed to the representationalist view of language. This view depends on an unexamined duality between world and words, between what exists and its expression. If something doesn't exist, then we shouldn't use a word for it, because that would be assuming it does exist. In non-dually correct representationalist speech, pronouns are out. Personal names such as Jason are harder to avoid. But some speakers do avoid them. Instead of saying "the body-mind organism called Jason," they might say "the body-mind organism *here*."

Something else strikes me about this kind of communication: it's unbalanced. It's not impartial or equal. It allows some things and disallows others. Jason wasn't avoiding absolutely every noun. In spite of his efforts not to refer to non-existent objects, he couldn't succeed completely. Certain things got a pass, such as bodies, minds, words, and coffee. Why weren't these words, which represent equally non-existent objects, avoided?

It has to do with where so many non-dual teachings place their emphasis. Most non-dual teachings work hard to demonstrate how the personal self doesn't exist. They deconstruct the personal self in many different ways, interpreting it as merely the result of a story, or as a label projected onto a body-mind mechanism. The personal self is the hot target of most teachings, as well it should be. But many non-dual teachings stop there. They may not deconstruct bodies, minds, or coffee. I've even known non-dualists who say that although the self doesn't exist, the body does.

Whenever we feel a sincere need to avoid common words for non-dually correct reasons, we're operating in the shadows of representationalism. We're accepting certain kinds of objective existence, even if only tacitly. This acceptance leaves a subtle sense of separation in its wake.

Nonreferentiality and the Direct Path

The direct path goes a different way. The direct path is egalitarian toward objects. It doesn't accept the objective existence of anything whatsoever, including awareness. Its approach to language is thoroughly nonreferential, breaking free of representationalism altogether.

How can you get comfortable with the nonreferential approach? One way is to see how representationalism doesn't make sense. Another way is to understand how you're already communicating nonreferentially, perhaps without knowing it. I'll discuss both.

Approaching Nonreferentiality Through Inquiry

As a student of the direct path, you come to see that representationalism's claims don't make sense. In your inquiry, you discover that these claims, which assume that objects exist in an independent way, are incoherent. You discover that in your direct experience, all objects (including words) are nothing more than arisings in witnessing awareness. There are simply no referents to be found. It's not just words for "awareness" that don't refer to an object. No word refers to any object in the way imagined by representationalism.

According to the direct path, all words refer or point to awareness alone. When a word arises, it occurs as a sound or visual mark. It arises from witnessing awareness, abides in awareness for a short while, and then subsides into awareness. The word's "home," its true meaning, is awareness. It embodies its true meaning not by representing awareness but by *being* awareness. Words are like any other object in this respect. Even when we seem to hear words, speak them, or understand them, these "events" are nothing more than arisings in awareness.

This balanced discovery about words and objects promotes a balanced attitude toward language. Since no object is found in direct experience, the "I" is on a par with the cup of coffee. Therefore, we don't need to outlaw certain words and allow others. All words fail to refer in the same way. We don't need to outlaw any words. We just use them differently.

We don't need to take the direct path's approach literally either. Imagine hearing this sentence:

Today will be cloudy with an 80 percent chance of precipitation.

Just because we've seen that words have their home in awareness doesn't require us to adopt a new literalism. We aren't obligated to translate the above sentence about the weather into "awareness talk":

Awareness awareness awareness awareness awareness awareness awareness awareness awareness awareness awareness.

With nonreferentiality, we have *more* freedom, not less. So I can write an e-mail message to a friend and communicate normally. I can say:

Hi, Jason. This is Greg Goode. We met at the Science and Non-duality Conference last year. I'll be in your area in two weeks. Would you like to get together for a cup of coffee?

Speaking in a natural, intuitive way, without having to force my everyday words to fit my spiritual teachings, brings the same wonderfully refreshing feeling of freedom as one experiences exploring poetry, humor, song, and dance. Our speech doesn't always have to conform to the cautious, factual, literal style of a police report.

In this section, I discussed the freedom of the nonreferential attitude toward language. I took the route of direct path–style inquiry, in which words and sentences are seen as appearances to witnessing awareness.

There's another route as well—attuning ourselves to the figurative aspects of language. Inquiry, although some people find it quite helpful, isn't required for this. In fact, this route may be more intuitive for those who don't relate strongly to doing inquiry. It involves looking through the lens of the artistic and rhetorical features of language itself. Shri Atmananda gives a hint about this in *Atma Darshan*. I examine this approach in the next section.

Approaching Nonreferentiality Through Figurative Language

The idea is to reach nonreferentiality through greater attention to figurative language. This is where poetry, literature, music, and even mythology come into play. Unlike literal language, figurative language doesn't assume that its referents exist. But it communicates nevertheless. The more you understand about how figurative language works, the more you'll use it knowingly, freely, and joyfully. (As I show toward the end of this chapter, even literal language can be seen as figurative.) In this section, I illustrate how to move closer and closer to using figurative language in a knowing way, as Shri Atmananda recommends.

In the preface to *Atma Darshan*, Shri Atmananda discusses the Vedantic Mahavakyas (Great Sayings) "That thou art" and "I am Brahman."[19] He recommends that when we contemplate one of these sayings in order to realize its truth, we set aside the literal meaning of key terms and take up what Indian philosophy of language calls the "indicatory" meaning. Other writers, including Swami Sivananda and the scholar Bimal Krishna Matilal, discuss these issues in much greater detail.[20]

What is "indicatory" meaning? According to Indian philosophy, "indicatory" comes from a word's *signifying* or *indicating* power. This is analogous to what in English we call the "figurative" meaning of a word. It's the basis for metaphor. When we focus on the figurative meaning instead of the literal meaning, we don't expect objective referents for our words. Our understanding can thus broaden.

When we apply figurative meaning to the Mahavakya, the literal meaning of "I am Brahman" is "I, Greg, am Brahman." The figurative meaning is "I, as awareness, am Brahman." According to the figurative meaning, I am awareness.

Amazing! If we simply switch to the figurative meaning of these terms, we're instantly carried past the normal limitations of our understanding and catapulted toward our goal. It requires no analysis or inquiry whatsoever! It's almost as if the literal meaning of the terms had itself created the illusion of separation.

As far as I can tell, people who discover these insights about figurative meaning feel a rush of relief and freedom. They feel as though their power of self-expression has been unleashed. They don't have to watch their words. If they're criticized by fans of the representationalist non-dual view, they can understand why this happens.

Some non-dual students have been told to stop reading books or to stop engaging with music, art, and film, especially works with non-spiritual topics. And then, if they actually do sneak in a novel or movie, they feel spiritual guilt. Of course the recommendation to put aside non-spiritual aesthetic material can certainly be effective for some people in the right circumstances. But to insist upon it for everyone becomes a kind of non-dual puritanism. If you can enjoy literature in a figurative, non-literal way, you don't have to reject it. You can use it in a new and beautifully poetic way. I say more about this below, beginning with simple examples.

Here's an example of literal meaning from Indian grammar:

The village is on the banks of the Ganges River.

Here's a very similar example, which uses non-literal, figurative meaning:

The village is on the Ganges River.

The village isn't literally *on* the river. The word "on" is figurative. But the sentence is so clear and straightforward, it seems to be literal!

There are many other ways that meaning can veer away from the literal. The more you can sensitize yourself to these variations in meaning, the less you'll feel attached to the literal meaning alone. Even though literal meaning isn't directly confirmed in the direct path, it still helps to become familiar with the varieties of non-literal meaning that you can choose from even now. You can enjoy greater freedom with this more open kind of communication.

Here are a few examples of non-literal meaning:

1. **Metaphoric meaning (similar to figurative meaning)**

    "It's raining men."

    Famously sung by The Weather Girls in 1982, "It's raining men" means the male-to-female ratio is advantageous for those who like men.

2. **Playful poetic meaning**

    "STIX NIX HIX PIX"

    This is the headline of a 1935 article about how audiences in rural areas (the STIX) tended to reject (NIX) films with rural settings (HIX PIX), preferring films about the urban upper class. This famous example of "slanguage," from the entertainment industry periodical *Variety*, served to support the periodical's view of itself as hip and superior, as being in the center of things.

3. **Nonsensical poetic meaning**

> 'Twas brillig, and the slithy toves
> > Did gyre and gimble in the wabe;
> All mimsy were the borogoves,
> > And the mome raths outgrabe.

> "Beware the Jabberwock, my son
> > The jaws that bite, the claws that catch!
> Beware the Jubjub bird, and shun
> > The frumious Bandersnatch!"

> He took his vorpal sword in hand;
> > Long time the manxome foe he sought—
> So rested he by the Tumtum tree,
> > And stood awhile in thought.

These are the first three stanzas of perhaps the most famous example of nonsensical poetic meaning, Lewis Carroll's "Jabberwocky" (1871). Their meaning is conveyed largely by sound and rhythm, not by dictionary or semantic meaning at all. Other examples are the vocal jazz scat singing of Jelly Roll Morton, Cab Calloway, and Ella Fitzgerald, and the melodic syllables heard in 1950s doo-wop songs such as "Mary Lee" by The Rainbows and "In the Still of the Night" by The Five Satins.

Well-crafted nonsense syllables sound just right. And in spite of their lack of semantic meaning, they're able to convey a tremendously strong sense that something important is being said. They can even bring to mind specific images and a feeling of agreement with what the speaker is (unconventionally) saying.

4. **Performative meaning**

"I now pronounce you husband and wife." Or "I promise to call you tomorrow."

These sentences don't pick out an objective meaning. They *establish* meaning by being uttered.

5. **Ironic meaning**

"How am I? Great! Just great! I was stuck in traffic this morning, I arrived late for work, and now I have a headache."

The speaker doesn't mean she's literally feeling great; quite the opposite.

There are many other types of non-literal meaning. All of them break free from the assumptions of the representationalist view, even if the speaker subscribes to that view. Even if you're a rigid representationalist, you can't control all the non-literal effects of your communication.

These different linguistic registers can be mixed. In fact, as your understanding improves, you'll be able to switch registers with increasing facility, sometimes even in the same sentence. For example, in the following sentence from *Notes on Spiritual Discourses of Shri Atmananda*, the word "you" switches senses twice, for a total of three types of meaning in eleven words!

Even when you say you are attached, you are really detached.[21]

1. "you say"

Literal, conventional meaning, in which Shri Atmananda is addressing the questioner in the questioner's own terms.

2. "you are attached"

This is cleverly and intentionally ambiguous. "You" carries two meanings at the same time: the implied literal meaning that the questioner applies to it, and the transcendent, impersonal meaning that Atmananda applies to it.

3. "you are really detached"

This is the figurative, transcendent meaning, in which "you" means witnessing awareness itself, not a person at all. Awareness is never attached to any object.

By recognizing these switches, or using them, you loosen your attachment to the representationalist view and its assumptions of objective existence and separation.

The Nonreferential Approach

The nonreferential approach to language doesn't do away with the idea of literal meaning. Nonreferentiality has its own take on literality. The meaning of "literal" transforms.

Even "Literal" Isn't Literal

What does "literal" even mean? Even the etymology doesn't support the representationalist view of language.

From the etymological perspective, the heart of literality isn't factuality, representation, or accuracy. The meaning pertains to expression, to letters. According to *Merriam-Webster's Unabridged Dictionary*, "literal" has several meanings. In the first meaning, "literal" refers to keeping with the letter of religious scriptures (as opposed to the "spirit" of the meaning). The second definition is the expected "adhering to fact." Factuality (a form of referentiality) does count as a meaning, but it isn't the first meaning listed. The primary definition of literal takes us first to words, not to their referents. The etymology of "literal" does the same thing. The word derives from Latin *littera* and *litera*, which mean "of a letter, of writing."

In this way, even the word "literal" is not literal but a metaphor. The original "letter" of "literal" has become a signifier for factuality. The letter is a metaphor for fact. In this case, literality is an effect of non-literality.

Literality is especially vulnerable to irony, the "bad boy" of figurative meaning. "Literal" as a word can become its own opposite, in which it means "not literal." When someone makes a big mistake at work, you might say: "When the boss finds out, heads will roll. Literally!" This irony was in place even two and a half centuries ago. In 1769, novelist Frances Brooke wrote the following passage in *The History of Emily Montague*: "He is a fortunate man to be introduced to such a party of fine women at his arrival; it is literally to feed among the lilies."

Literality Divided Against Itself

Literality is also subject to contradictory meanings. Sometimes a word can have opposing literal meanings. Such words are called auto-antonyms, antagonyms, or contronyms. For example, the word "sanction" means both to impose a penalty upon and also to give approval to. The word "cleave" means both to cling or adhere to and also to split or sever.

So how can we think of literal meaning? After all, literality as imagined by the representationalist as a word-world correspondence doesn't make sense. We're never in a position to stand aside from words and the world so that we can measure the degree of fit or correspondence. This model gives us no way to perform the required tests.

So if this meaning of literality doesn't make sense, doesn't the idea of figurative language also lose its sense? How can there be figurative meaning without literal meaning? Doesn't the distinction melt away?

Even though the literal/figurative distinction isn't something we directly experience as existing in the objective sense, we don't have to discard it in practice. As a nonreferentialist, I can still see pragmatic value in distinguishing some kinds of communication from others. Human communication is vast, with lots of different styles and purposes. A medical textbook uses language in a different way than does a poem, a novel, or a street-corner conversation. So why not retain the literal/figurative distinction, though without trying to base the difference on a correspondence to objective reality?

One way to retain the distinction is to see "literal" and "figurative" as being based on different communicative styles or conventions. For example, we may see literal meaning as what happens when old metaphors become stale or where there's widespread agreement about a word or sentence. "The arm of my chair is broken." We may think of literal meaning as how police reports communicate. We can see figurative meaning coming from newer metaphors or perhaps from contexts in which there's less agreement or a greater spirit of play. "She led the radical arm of her English class." We may think of figurative meaning as how poetry and song and slang and jokes communicate.

Stories of Nonreferentiality

Here are two stories that illustrate how nonreferentiality can help us enjoy and understand life more fully. In my experience, the more I'm attuned to nonreferentiality, the more freedom I have to embrace life in creative new ways.

The Jury-Duty Story

About a year ago, I was called to jury duty. Many people who are called are unable to actually serve on a jury for various reasons, including imminent plans to travel or have surgery. In a culturally diverse area such as New York City, there's another frequent reason that people can't serve: inability to understand the language of the court (English, in this case).

I arrived on a Monday. There were almost a thousand of us sitting in the assembly hall. A uniformed federal marshal came to the microphone and made some announcements over the loudspeaker. At one point he announced very seriously, "All of you who are under age eighteen or who do not understand English are excused."

When I heard this, I couldn't hold back my laughter. If listeners could understand this sentence enough to get up to leave the room, then they ought to stay in the room! On the other hand, if they didn't understand English and should therefore be excused, they wouldn't be able to understand the sentence in the first place!

By opening myself to non-literal meaning, I was able to experience a bit of humor and joy. These benefits come from the poetic and literary alternatives to literal meaning. We're free to interpret in this way as well as literally and in non-dually "correct" terms as "awareness awareness."

Religious, spiritual, and literary utterances are particularly hard to pin down. There might be practical, historical, or textual reasons for one interpretation or another, but we can never specify these things fully. There can be no end to the factors that might change our assessment. Any seemingly literal utterance could be a quote, a joke, a poem, or part of a play or dream. No formula can specify with 100 percent certainty the type of meaning that a sentence "really" has. For example, what do we do with sentences like the following?

"My guru arrived last night. We're so psyched! The whole town is on fire!"

On fire? The speaker is probably talking about enthusiasm for his guru. The literal meaning wouldn't make sense, would it? Is the guru a pyromaniac? Literal meaning is often our first hypothesis. If that would lead to an unlikely interpretation, then we check for the possibility of figurative meaning, which may make more sense in the context. Neither meaning is immediately given. We have to search and check and negotiate in order to arrive at the meaning we give the sentence.

Here's a similar case:

"My path is the highest teaching."

This also seems literal, but it's another metaphor. "Higher" indicates "true" or "final," not farther from Earth's surface. If we see this as a metaphorical phrase, we can see the speaker's statement not as an empirical truth about spiritual teachings in and of themselves but as the speaker's desire to elevate his own teaching over others. "Highest" can be seen as a metaphor for the speaker's conviction. Appreciating language in this way serves to free us from the speaker's claims of absolute superiority!

The Satsang Teacher Story

The other story of nonreferentiality is a case in which literal and non-literal meanings directly oppose each other. If you open up to the non-literal meaning, you'll discover helpful new ways of thinking about things in the everyday sense.

I'll illustrate this with a generic example that I have seen played out many times, even as early as the 1990s. Back then, *satsang* was taught by an exclusive few, who never got up in front of people without reporting their membership in a spiritual lineage stretching back to Ramana Maharshi or Nisargadatta Maharaj. Among *satsang* students, the most valued goal was to become a teacher. The process of becoming a teacher was surrounded by mystery, celebrity, and excitement.

Imagine attending a *satsang* the way they were back in the 1990s: The teacher sits on a plush armchair at the front of the room, while audience members sit on hard folding chairs. On a table next to the teacher is a row of three or four framed photos, showing a progression of spiritual teachers starting with Ramana Maharshi and ending with the very person sitting in the armchair. Imagine the *satsang* beginning with the teacher saying the following:

This is not about me. You may look at me sitting in this chair up here in the front and wonder why I am here and you are not. I am just like you. Even though I am up here and you are not, it doesn't mean that I am special.

I don't even consider myself to be a teacher. I never wanted to teach. It was my teacher who asked me to teach. He gave me the gift of *satsang*, and I am here giving it to you.

The gift of freedom in *satsang* is the highest gift that can be given. It is the most intense form of love and the most profound happiness imaginable. I wish to share it with you.

This is a classic example of non-literal meaning contradicting literal meaning in a way that rhetoricians call *apophasis*, or "affirming by denying" (illustrated by the popular phrase "If you deny it, you supply it"). When a candidate for political office says, "And I won't mention my opponent's financial problems," you know what's coming next!

In our example of the *satsang* monologue, the literal interpretation of the teacher's opening statements is that he's just like his audience members.

But everything else about the situation—from the seating arrangements, to the row of photos, to the teacher's self-consciousness as a giver of *satsang*, to his disavowal of teacher status—tells a different story. The teacher's very first sentence isn't about the audience or about the official *satsang* topics of consciousness or enlightenment. It's about *him*. He goes on to mention himself a total of thirteen times in eleven sentences. The focus is squarely on him, and, according to the non-literal meaning of his speech, he emerges not the same as others, but very different indeed. He becomes the teacher who has been specially selected to bear the most precious gift of all. This is a case in which being open to non-literal meaning provides access to a deeper and more subtle understanding of a situation.

What Else Can You Do?

If you're interested in the linguistic approach to nonreferentiality, you can expand upon Shri Atmananda's advice. You can be open to as many non-literal linguistic nuances as you can. You can try to see the non-literal in the literal. You can relax around the demand you feel to land on the "true" meaning of an utterance. In fact, the very effort to figure out the "true" meaning of a sentence is a throwback to the representationalist way of thinking!

You can cultivate an enjoyment of poetry, drama, lyrics, literature, music, film, and art without limiting yourself to officially "spiritual" topics. Your heart will open wider if you stop trying to be narrow in your choice of material. In fact, when you're able to engage with these things nonreferentially, you'll be better able to see the "spiritual" in the "non-spiritual." This is a delightful, playful, heart-opening way to go about spirituality. You may find it especially welcome if you don't relate very well to the method of inquiry, because you can do it without any logic or inquiry. As you enjoy a fuller range of linguistic nuance, you'll become more flexible around language and conceptuality, more playful and creative, and less referential.

Imagination

Imagination is rarely mentioned in non-dual teachings. If you're on a non-dual path, perhaps you think you're being more serious, accurate, and realistic if you don't indulge your imagination.

Over the years, in speaking with many people about these issues, I've come to think that lack of imagination may contribute to attachment to the literal view of language. I've noticed that people have an easier time with non-dual teachings when they've had deep involvement in music, literature, film, historical fiction or science fiction, esoteric cosmologies, Eastern psychologies, or tantric visualization. These require a kind of openness that goes at least a little beyond the literal-mindedness of the representationalist.

These activities involve playing with figurative language, metaphor, metonymy, synecdoche, irony, poetry, nonsense, and performativity. It includes storytelling, literature, mythology, history, sociology—even comic books and vampire stories. Engaging these different worldviews and uses of language lessens people's feeling that literalism tells the truth about things.

Truth, Falsity, and the Writing of This Chapter

All this talk about nonreferentiality might prompt you to ask: "Okay, so what about truth and falsity? If we can't rely on the idea of correspondence to reality, are truth and falsity totally out the door?"

This is a very good question. Actually, the question of truth, along with the related issues of conceptuality and thought, is investigated in the direct path.[22] In one sense, truth is Being, and Being is our very nature. It's not that some sentences express truth. It's that truth is an aspect of awareness—our nature—and it is what everything already is.

And when it comes to doing inquiry, you directly experience sentences and concepts as arisings in awareness. Of course, being arisings in awareness, they're inseparable from awareness, which, again, has the aspect of the truth of our Being. Traditionally, the word is even capitalized, "Truth"! In inquiry, you never experience sentences as referring to anything external to the global awareness from which they arise. As an inheritance from Vedanta, the direct path sometimes speaks of awareness as Truth and Being and Knowledge and Love. These are inspiring poetic equivalences of awareness itself.

For this reason, the direct path offers no official doctrine of everyday truth. As a student of the direct path, you don't need to think in a certain way about truth, as long as your ideas about truth don't make you feel like a separate or alienated individual entity in a world of separate things. To become free of these kinds of separation, you inquire into the idea of objective truth and find no support for the idea. You're freed from expecting "true" sentences to bridge a gap between the mind and the world. It's only a gap created by unexamined assumptions. Inquiry clarifies all this. You then discover that living and acting take care of themselves in a wonderfully spontaneous way. No theory of truth is needed.

But there *are* nonreferential notions of truth. They keep the everyday distinction between truth and falsity, but they don't liken truth to verbal correspondence with reality. One notion of truth that's compatible with the nonreferentiality of the direct path is the "coherence theory."[23] It's not a perfect fit with the direct path, but it avoids the assumptions about truly existent objects that one finds in representationalism.

According to the coherence theory, a true statement is one that coheres or agrees to a great extent with other statements that we believe, whereas a false statement is one that doesn't agree very well.

The coherence theory makes a powerful point: coherence is how we test for truth, even for representationalists, who believe that truth is correspondence between sentences and rocks. That is, even representationalists end up testing the truth of sentences by assessing how well a new sentence agrees with current sentences in their belief system. Some of the sentences might be "about" external objects and might refer to sensory evidence. But in their test of truth, representationalists still end up comparing sentences and sense impressions for coherence with each other. No one ever works directly with the external objects, even if they believe in them. The coherence theorist says that this kind of pragmatic coherence assessment not only is how everyone tests for truth but also serves as the meaning of truth. We simply have no need, argues the coherence theorist, to assert that our sentences correspond to objects in the world.

The coherence theorist makes another important point about the correspondence theory of truth: Just how is correspondence supposed to work, anyway? How does a sentence about a rock sitting by a tree actually correspond to the rock and the tree? What kind of equivalences are we supposed to draw between the sentence (sounds or marks) and the objective rock and tree? And how are we to assess the degree of correspondence? According to the coherence theorist, the burden of proof lies on correspondence theorists to give an account of these features of their theory, which is all the more important because they're using it to substantiate metaphysical claims of true existence.

In addition to wondering about notions of truth and falsity, you might wonder whether I really mean what I say when I talk about language in this chapter. Am I making truth claims that are supposed to represent reality? Am I somehow violating the insights I'm talking about? For example, am I giving a literalist explanation of literal and figurative language? Am I giving a representationalist account of the difference between representationalism and nonreferentiality?

These are important questions to consider whenever a conversation on non-duality turns to topics of language or communication. So much of our non-dual talk eventually comes to the subject of talking itself. So in the case of this chapter, what perspective is all the talk coming from?

My approach is this. I'm writing this chapter—indeed, this entire book—from a deeply happy sense of joyful irony, which is covered in more detail in the next section, as well as in chapter 10, "After Awareness: The End of the Path." I don't see my words—or any other sets of words, for that matter—as trying to represent reality or as being objectively true.

It might seem that I'm obligated to tell an objectively true counter-story as an alternative to the standard representationalist story I'm deconstructing. But that's just my point: I can't do that. It would be self-refuting to try. As a nonreferentialist, I'm not assuming that words or languages exist either outside or inside of awareness. I don't even think of awareness as a container with boundaries or sides. One way to talk about my words in this chapter would be this: I can visualize you and me rowing boats on a smooth lake. I'm rowing a boat next to yours, making ripples in the water. Some of my ripples may move your boat slightly, inspiring you to look at things in a more freeing way.

Joyful Irony

Nonreferentiality helps you get to what I like to call "joyful irony."

Joyful irony, based loosely on an idea from Richard Rorty (1931–2007), is a bundle of attitudes and freedoms that you discover when the direct path is working as advertised. The "joy" stands for freedom from suffering, freedom from belief and conceptuality, and the freedom of openheartedness toward the world. The "irony" stands for freedom from the set of views that claim that language is supposed to mirror the world. Freedom from this view of language brings several other freedoms: freedom from the realist representationalism of language, freedom from dogmatism, freedom to interact with more people, and freedom from being right or wrong about reality in and of itself.

Perhaps the most important point is that joyful irony starts at home. Your own nonreferential attitude toward language begins with insight about *your own* favorite vocabulary, not *someone else's*. You branch out from there. Realizing that not even your own favorite words and concepts can be taken literally in the representationalist sense transforms your thinking about all words and concepts. You stop thinking of yourself as "right" about things, and you can no longer consider other people "wrong." In joyful irony, the dualistic structures and assumptions about all views evaporate into freedom, love, and humor. Beginning with your own, you can't argue about the superiority of spiritual paths.

Joyful irony doesn't mean that "anything goes." The joyful ironist doesn't avoid love, compassion, manners, ethics, or other norms and standards. The joyful ironist doesn't morph into a mad bomber or a Ponzi schemer. This is due to the "joy" in joyful irony: the loving engagement with the world that doesn't treat the speaker as privileged over others. The "irony" in joyful irony is that you don't believe thoughts. You don't interpret thoughts, words, or concepts, especially your own, as true representations of reality. In your actions and day-to-day living, there might be a consistent type of engagement that looks to others as if you are following objective standards. But you're not. Your engagement happens spontaneously, in total freedom from the assumption that standards are hardwired into reality. This is also the "irony."

Getting Beyond Words

Nonreferentiality is another way of getting beyond words. Someone reading this chapter might object that all this emphasis on language keeps us trapped at the level of words, whereas the purpose of any spiritual path is to take us beyond words.

But being "beyond words" doesn't necessitate a phenomenal silence or a literal absence of words. In fact, getting beyond words is accomplished by nonreferentiality itself. The more we become sensitive to the ways of non-literal meaning, the more we open ourselves to a vast space of clarity that is unlimited by language, reference, logic, and conceptuality.

CHAPTER 4

The Guru Doctrine

Dear Greg,

I have heard that one must have personal contact with a living guru in order to reach enlightenment. Shri Atmananda says so many times in *Notes on Spiritual Discourses of Shri Atmananda*. But I live in Plovdiv, Bulgaria. I don't have much money, and it's not easy for me to travel to see teachers. So I read books and watch videos on the Internet. Is this enough? Do I have a chance?

This chapter isn't about the overall topic of the guru in the direct path. Instead, it seeks to address the very specific question asked above: "Is personal contact with a living guru necessary for enlightenment?" This question comes up for many followers of the direct path. For others, it isn't an issue at all. If you're among the latter, feel free to skip this chapter.

Over the years, I've received many entreaties like the one above. People really want reassurance that freedom is within reach and not made impossible by distance or finances. In most varieties of modern non-dual teachings, personal contact with a living guru isn't a requirement. But for those inspired by the direct path of Shri Atmananda, the issue comes up from time to time because of what's said in *Notes on Spiritual Discourses of Shri Atmananda*.

For current teachers of the direct path, this hasn't been an issue. Even though Shri Atmananda never publicly designated a successor, all the direct-path teachers, as far as I know, have had this kind of connection with a living guru. Western teachers who were students of Shri Atmananda include Wolter Keers, John Levy, and Jean Klein. Jean served as the teacher for Francis Lucille, among others. Francis has been my teacher and Rupert Spira's. No one who teaches under the auspices of the direct path will tell you "Personal contact with a living guru isn't necessary; I didn't need it and neither do you." At the same time, I'm not aware of any direct-path teacher who would tell you "Personal contact with a living guru is absolutely necessary; no one has any hope without it."

So is it necessary or not?

In a nutshell, I interpret the insistence upon a guru as a kind of *prakriya*, or "teaching method." But before going into detail about the question of the guru's necessity, I'd like to look into some background on this particular teaching. Where does it come from, this emphasis on the personal connection with a living guru? Primarily it comes from *Notes*.

The emphasis on the guru takes a strong form in *Notes*, which is why our Bulgarian friend wrote to me in the first place. According to the strong form of this teaching, personal contact with the guru is a necessity for self-realization. I'll call this claim the "guru doctrine." The guru doctrine comes across in Shri Atmananda's talks themselves but is conveyed perhaps even more insistently in the supporting material written by *Notes* compiler and editor Nitya Tripta. Tripta is the author of a short chapter in *Notes* called "On Devotion to a Living Guru." In a section called "Need of a Guru (and Danger of More Than One)," Tripta discusses the necessity of the Karana-guru. *Karana* comes from the Sanskrit word *karanam* ("reason" or "cause"). Karana-guru is a term used by Shri Atmananda for the guru who's established in the Truth and who's able to cause the student to visualize this same Truth. Tripta writes that

> [Shri Atmananda] asserted most emphatically that no aspirant, however great, could ever attain liberation without the help of a Karana-guru *in person*.[24]

Contact isn't necessarily a matter of words. It can be non-verbal, as Tripta explains.

> This Karana-guru in person is indispensable for Self-realization, though in some very mature cases of *uttamadhikaris* the contact might be only for a few seconds, by a word or a touch or even a look.[25]

Shri Atmananda is considerably more nuanced in his approach to the guru doctrine. He doesn't mention it in every single one of his talks. He mentions the importance of the guru in response to particular questions from beginners or in contexts in which it seems that self-inquiry isn't the preferred method of attaining self-knowledge. I'll come back to this point later in this chapter.

The guru doctrine makes a particular kind of logical claim, stressing the absolute necessity of face-to-face contact with a living human guru. This is a much stronger claim than merely saying that a guru is helpful or useful in reaching self-realization.

There's no doubt that a guru can be helpful. The guru can personalize spiritual teachings in a skillful way that makes them intuitive for a particular person. The guru can respond in a flexible way to a seeker's deepest and most idiosyncratic questions, whereas a book or video can't.

But is the stronger claim true? Is it impossible for an aspirant to reach self-knowledge without direct contact with a living human guru? And does Shri Atmananda really mean to assert this as a principle that applies to all aspirants everywhere?

Gurus vs. Books

According to several of Shri Atmananda's statements in *Notes*, the aspirant receives something essential and mysterious from the guru: love, light, and the force of truth,[26] and these qualities, which only the guru possesses, are more transformational than mere words. When the student sees the guru not as a person but as the Truth beyond phenomenality, the student's ego and sense of embodiment disappear, and he or she can visualize the Truth directly. Shri Atmananda says:

> But the disciple, as long as he feels himself embodied, sees the Guru only as a personality. Slowly, the disciple realizes that he is that living principle beyond the body, senses and mind. Then he finds the Guru also correspondingly exalted.
>
> At last, when the disciple, taken thus to the brink of the mind, listens to the words of the Guru explaining the nature of the positive Self, he is suddenly thrown into that supreme experience of the ultimate. It is only then that he realizes the state of the Guru to be that always, whether in apparent activity or inactivity. Thus alone can Truth be ever realized.[27]

Reading books alone won't help, according to Shri Atmananda. Unless you've met the guru and heard the Truth expounded, the force of Truth won't be present. Books can't provide that experience of egolessness that allows the Truth to be visualized.

> When you listen to the spoken word of the Guru, even on the first occasion your ego takes leave of you and you visualize the Truth at once, being left alone in your real nature. But when you read the same words by yourself, your ego lingers on in the form of the word, its meaning, etc., and you fail to transcend them. To visualize the Truth, the only condition needed is the elimination of the ego. *This is never possible by mere reading, before meeting the Guru.*[28]

Shri Atmananda sometimes expressed very conservative attitudes toward reading. When asked by a doctor what philosophy books to read, Atmananda replied:

> A Sage alone can show you the Truth. But after understanding the Truth from the Sage, you may read only the few books he suggests, to keep you in the groove he has chalked out. After some time, when you are established in the Truth yourself, you may read any book, good or bad.[29]

I'll return to the issue of reading and books a bit later as well.

The Guru Doctrine vs. Bhakti Yoga

Although the guru stands at the center of both concepts, Shri Atmananda promotes only the guru doctrine, not bhakti yoga.

The guru doctrine only requires you to hear the Truth expounded by the guru. It doesn't require you to worship the guru, as does bhakti yoga. Actually, Shri Atmananda was a proponent of self-inquiry and cautioned against bhakti yoga for most people. However, for those already doing bhakti yoga, he recommends that

> you attach greater reality to the Lord in your vision than to the objects of this gross world. The more you emphasize the Lord, you are indirectly and unknowingly emphasizing your own personal self as the perceiver. This can never be a help to the attainment of the impersonal.
>
> It is the experience of all Sages who have had dualistic *bhakti* or yogic training in their early days that all that training had really been, in one sense, an obstacle to their progress to the ultimate Truth.[30]

So if you don't already practice bhakti yoga, you have no obligation to begin practicing it. Atmananda's point is rather that if you *do* happen to be devotionally inclined, the object of your devotion matters. Your bhakti energies should be directed not toward deities such as Krishna or Shiva but rather toward the guru or toward consciousness itself. According to Shri Atmananda,

> a real devotee can only and need only direct his attention to the Consciousness in him. This is real *bhakti*; and it immediately yields Peace or *ananda*, which is Consciousness itself… *Bhakti* for anything other than this is really unworthy of the name. It may, at the most, be called a fascination as unreal as the object itself.[31]

There are times when Shri Atmananda recommended the aspirant focus on the guru as a main practice. These included cases in which consciousness and contemplation would be too abstract for the person. Here's a letter from Atmananda to a thirteen-year-old student he called Ponnu, who was a Krishna devotee. He stresses the importance of the guru and the importance of not having more than one.

Peace thou be,

Letter received. The *unconditioned love towards one's own Guru* is the only ladder to the goal of Truth. That *prema-bhakti is not something which could be shared*. No other kind of love or devotion should be capable of bearing comparison to it. A disciple should never bow allegiance to two Gurus at the same time.

May the Lord Bhagavan who is the embodiment of *sat-citananda* abide in Ponnu for ever.

With love and blessings

(signed)

P. Krishna Menon[32]

Self-Realization According to the Guru Doctrine

According to the guru doctrine, the process of self-realization may be divided informally into four stages.

1. **Contact.** Whether you read books, cultivate spiritual practices, or begin merely with an interest, you should at some point come into personal contact with a Karana-guru. You may need the entire exposition of the truth from beginning to end (which is called *tattvopadesha*). Or, depending on your readiness, you may need just a few words or a glance.

Tattvopadesha carries an extra power. This is the unassailable logic that forces you beyond the usual personal perspective and compels your focus into the perspective of the Absolute.

2. **Visualization.** You're made to feel something magical that escapes your ability to describe. This wordless magical feeling will assist in your visualization of your true nature.

3. **Stabilization.** You might need to apply some effort. After your moment of visualization with the guru, you need to "cling on to the Truth so visualized."[33] You may do this by listening to the guru again, as well as by visualizing the Truth over and over. Or you may go over the arguments heard from the guru, or parallel arguments. You may also read books by the guru containing similar arguments. These arguments can take you to the same Truth you experienced in the guru's presence. Go over them again and again.

4. **Establishment.** Through your stabilizing efforts, your knowledge of the Truth of your being becomes unshakable. Your old perspective, in which you misinterpreted the "I" as the mind or body, evaporates. Your new perspective becomes established, in which the self becomes the self of all. The self is realized as awareness.

So according to the guru doctrine, it's imperative for the seeker to come into contact with a living guru. Without this contact, self-realization is impossible.

The Other Atmananda

A much different picture emerges if we look at Shri Atmananda's other works. Besides *Notes*, his most relevant works available in English are *Atma Darshan*, *Atma Nirvriti*, *Atmananda Tattwa Samhita*,[34] and his commentary on *Ashtavakra Samhita*.[35] In fact, *Notes* is a publication that doesn't even carry Shri Atmananda's byline. The only byline is Nitya Tripta's.[36] (The other works do carry Atmananda's byline.)

The Guru Doctrine Is Never Mentioned

In these other works, the guru doctrine is never articulated. There's ample opportunity in all of these works to mention it. But we simply don't find it in works other than *Notes*. This would be a stunningly irresponsible omission if contact with the guru were actually indispensable for self-realization.

The reason for the difference, it seems, is that Shri Atmananda stressed the necessity of the guru *in person* but not *in writing*. In his written works, Atmananda never mentions the guru doctrine, and in one case (to be examined below) he even challenges it.

And even in spoken communication, he doesn't always mention the guru doctrine. For example, in the lesser-known set of dialogues *Atmananda Tattwa Samhita*, the guru doctrine is never mentioned. This work, edited by Shri Atmananda's son Shri Adwayananda, is a transcription of recorded talks with advanced disciples. It even contains an entire chapter on the guru-disciple relationship. The purpose of this conversation is to clarify the true meaning of the guru-disciple relationship. It explores this notion by shuttling back and forth between relative and absolute perspectives. But nowhere in the chapter is it stated or even hinted that personal contact with the guru is necessary for self-realization. The section titled "Life Sketch" and other matter contributed by the editor similarly make no mention of the necessity of personal contact.

But it's in Shri Atmananda's written work that the omission of the guru principle becomes most significant. *Atma Darshan* and *Atma Nirvriti* are his best-known written works. Composed in Malayalam using *sloka*-like verses that read like sutras, these two booklets are among the most deeply insightful Advaitic works ever written. They were even translated into English by Shri Atmananda himself.

But the guru doctrine isn't mentioned in either of these works. Shri Atmananda doesn't even mention it in either book's preface, in which he talks about the book and sets forth his purpose in writing it. He never says, "This is only a summary of the teaching. To make it really work for you, you must go see a guru in person so that you can be made to visualize the Truth."

The word "guru" does occur one time in *Atma Nirvriti* (20:VII), but in a way that almost makes the guru seem superfluous. It's never stated that the seeker needs a special form of communication that's only available through personal contact. The text makes it clear that the seeker is already standing in the Truth and just needs reminding. The chapter itself accomplishes the reminding.

Other Methods Are Given as Sufficient for Self-Realization

Not only do Shri Atmananda's written works fail to mention the guru principle, they also provide several *other* methods that are given as sufficient for realizing the truth. Chapters 10 and 12 of *Atma Darshan* recommend *discrimination, analysis,* and *contemplation.*[37] For example, with discrimination (called *viveka* in traditional Vedanta), you intuitively recognize the essential difference between subject and object, seer and seen, permanent and passing, awareness and the objects that appear to awareness.

Discrimination, analysis, and contemplation aren't merely theoretical or intellectual; they belong to the overall process that Atmananda calls "higher reason" (which he provides traditional Vedantic terms for: *vidya-vritti* or *viveka-vritti*).[38] Higher reason is "reason" because it proceeds similarly to logic and inference. It's "higher" because its source is awareness itself. It transcends the mind. In higher reason, premises are not learned concepts but the experiences of your own being, which can't seem unreasonable. The conclusion of higher reasoning is a non-conceptual knowledge of your true nature. Higher reason allows you to do self-inquiry without getting caught in the logical paradox of a mind trying to realize its own unreality. That would be like a knife trying to cut itself. Because higher reason emanates from a source beyond the mind, it can examine the mind to discover its true nature.

The preface to *Atma Nirvriti* is particularly meaningful in its wholehearted endorsement of *texts* as helpful in realizing the truth.[39] The preface encourages the study of *Atma Nirvriti* so that the aspirant may stabilize the knowledge of the truth gained through earlier study of *Atma Darshan*. Study of *Atma Nirvriti* is recommended so that knowledge of one's nature will become unshakable, which in turn will result in the attainment of lasting peace. If Shri Atmananda thought a face-to-face encounter with the guru were necessary, the preface would be the ideal place to say so. But he didn't say so. How could Shri Atmananda fail to mention this if it's as important as Nitya Tripta says?

The Guru Doctrine Is Challenged

In one of his works, a short commentary on *Ashtavakra Samhita*, Shri Atmananda comes very close to directly refuting the guru principle. As far as I know, this commentary has never been published or publicly disseminated. Instead, it has only been privately circulated among Atmananda's students. This short work consists of a tiny introduction by Shri Atmananda followed by verses of *Ashtavakra Samhita* in English. After many of the verses, Atmananda inserts his own commentary.

Shri Atmananda uses the English translation of *Ashtavakra Samhita* by Swami Nityaswarupananda (1899–1992) of the Sri Ramakrishna Math.[40] The Swami Nityaswarupananda edition features its own substantial introduction, which may have been written by Swami Nityaswarupananda himself.

Swami Nityaswarupananda's introduction cautions the reader not to interpret *Ashtavakra Samhita* or Vedanta as mere intellectual philosophy. Vedanta uses philosophy, yes, but it's able to transcend mere intellectuality by means of a "supra-rational organon called self-realization, which directly intuits the Truth."[41] This "supra-rational organon" is very similar to Atmananda's "higher reason."

It's in Shri Atmananda's own introduction to his *Ashtavakra Samhita* commentary that he takes issue with the guru principle. First, he quotes from Swami Nityaswarupananda's introduction, which assumes a version of the guru principle, saying that "the spiritual aspirant must undergo a course of Sadhana under the guidance and supervision of the Guru, who has himself gone through the grind and envisaged the Truth face to face."[42]

Then Atmananda says that, although the classic view is that there's a need to do *sadhana* with a guru (as Swami Nityaswarupananda asserts), in the direct path, there's no need to work with a guru and do *sadhana*. All you need is higher reason. With higher reason, you transcend the normal limits of intellectual reason, because you directly intuit the truth. Higher reason is sufficient.

The Presence of the Guru in Speech vs. Writing

There's no doubt that the Shri Atmananda of *Notes* asserts the guru principle. And there's no doubt that the Atmananda of *Atma Darshan*, *Atma Nirvriti*, and the *Ashtavakra Samhita* commentary doesn't endorse the guru principle. In fact, in these three works, he actually provides other means to self-realization that he states as sufficient.

It appears that Shri Atmananda didn't interpret the principle the same way as Nitya Tripta did. Tripta's "Life Sketch" of Shri Atmananda at the end of *Notes* offers a bibliography. Discussing *Atma Darshan* as a book, Tripta says:

A close study of this book, even by an ordinary aspirant, enables him to have an indirect knowledge of Atma, the Self. This indirect knowledge of the Truth in turn intensifies his earnestness and sincerity to know the Truth directly, and thus transforms him into a genuine *jijnyasu* or a true aspirant, thereby guaranteeing the attainment of a Karana-guru and liberation.[43]

This passage makes a distinction between *indirect* knowledge of the self that we attain through studying *Atma Darshan* and *direct* knowledge of the self that comes through a Karana-guru. But this distinction isn't made anywhere in *Atma Darshan*. Why not? If Shri Atmananda thought that the book was to be merely a springboard to a Karana-guru, he didn't say so in the book.

Instead, the sense we get from a close study of *Atma Darshan* is that the book itself is self-sufficient. *Atma Darshan* doesn't teach us about the Self. It doesn't give us indirect factual or philosophical knowledge. Rather, it invites us to do the inquiries and reminders provided by the text. These inquiries are brilliant portals to direct experience. It's through these direct means that we're able to know the self in a direct way. What takes place is much more than just reading.

Another way to look at the guru-versus-book issue is this. Why can't the Karana-guru be the book itself? Can't the author appear in literary form?

There's a kind of rich rhetorical irony here. The guru principle stresses face-to-face contact with the guru. And as we see in *Notes*, the principle is itself communicated face-to-face. The medium in which the guru principle is most frequently not asserted, and even perhaps denied, is *writing*. The irony is that each rhetorical mode tends to bring its own authority to the forefront and place the other mode in the background. We don't find Shri Atmananda *talking* about the authority of *writing*, or *writing* about the authority of *talking*. Such ironies often emerge in communication.

We can honor Shri Atmananda's legacy by honoring either mode of communication. So for the seeker who reads all of Atmananda's available texts, both possibilities are present. This brings us back to our original question.

Back to Bulgaria

Our Bulgarian friend asked in so many words, "Is it really true that I must have personal contact with a living guru in order to reach enlightenment?" In view of everything we've discussed here, I suggest that this isn't a clear or helpful question. I would recommend a more reasonable and practical question instead: "Would working with a guru be helpful in *my* search to realize the truth?" This question is much easier to answer. In fact, there's a helpful irony with this question. The more important the question seems to the person asking it, the more affirmative the answer.

A guru will be helpful for all the usual reasons that teachers are helpful. A guru can provide individualized help and recommendations, as well as inspiration. The guru can serve as a living, breathing example of the truth of the teaching.

So what about Shri Atmananda's teachings about the special love, light, and force of Truth that emanate from the guru in person? There are many ways to look at this. One person's beloved guru may be another person's boring old windbag. Or, perhaps the love, light, and force of Truth can come through a one-on-one video chat. Or how about a text? Some people are able to feel love, light, and the force of Truth coming quite strongly from the words in *Atma Darshan* and *Atma Nirvriti*. Why should this be impossible, especially when, according to the direct path, all words are appearances in awareness? Perhaps the two parties don't even have to be connected through visual means at all. For example, practices such as remote viewing and energetic healing can be performed at a distance. Perhaps the truth can be communicated in this way too.

Some people might require more face-to-face assistance than others. Because of this, and because Shri Atmananda articulates different approaches in different places, I like to interpret the guru doctrine as one particular teaching method among others. So I think that our Bulgarian friend's chances are quite good!

CHAPTER 5

Alternatives to Inquiry

Although the direct path has a reputation for being intellectual, it offers a surprising number of non-intellectual activities and experiments. In this chapter, we'll look at these other activities.

The reputation for intellectuality is probably due to the direct path's emphasis on inquiry, which uses reasoning and insight. In direct-path inquiry, you use a combination of direct experience and reasoning to inquire into the world, the body, and the mind. The result is a radical gestalt shift, a change in perspective. You stop identifying as a mind, a body, or a person, and you begin to identify as awareness before ceasing to identify altogether. When this teaching is set forth in its entirety, either by a teacher or in a book such as *The Direct Path: A User Guide*, it's called *tattvopadesha* ("teaching on reality").

The process of working through these inquiries does involve cognitive resources, and it can make the path seem dry and philosophical. Not everyone relates to that approach.

But many other spiritual approaches in the direct path don't use this kind of inquiry. These other approaches are used most often when teachers work directly with students. If you attend a retreat, for example, you stand a very good chance of encountering these other methods.

- Karma yoga

- Bhakti yoga

- Reminders

- Standing as awareness

- The Heart Opener

- Sleeping Knowingly

- Guided meditations

- The Yoga of Awareness

The Direct Method vs. the Upanishadic Method

According to the direct path, what makes it "direct" is that it doesn't try to move or change or create or eradicate anything. Students of the direct path don't become anything new or discard anything old. The direct path proposes no creation stories about the world and gives no causal explanations as to why things seem to be a certain way. It doesn't try to get you to ascend to higher and higher levels of reality. It doesn't have you try to better your individual thoughts and feelings so that only pleasant or impressive ones arise. Instead, it begins by taking you as you are. It directs your attention to the clarity, love, and truth of your direct experience, and then it proceeds from there. You discover global clarity. Even the moments that previously seemed to prove the truth of duality, you discover, are seamless clarity.

Shri Atmananda explains this "direct method" by distinguishing it from what he calls the traditional Upanishadic method:

All Upanishadic methods try to eliminate you from the *anatma*, and to establish you in the Atma.

But here, according to the direct method, you are shown that you can never get away either from your own shadow or from your reality. You are only asked to look deep into what you call *anatma*, and see beyond the shadow of a doubt that it is nothing but Atma—the Reality.[44]

The difference, as Shri Atmananda sees it, is that the Upanishadic methods try to dispel ignorance and establish you in the truth, whereas in the direct method you look at *anatma* ("not-self") and understand that it was already the self. There's nothing to eliminate, nothing to become, and nothing that you need to establish yourself in.[45] Because what we think of as the "not-self" is already Reality, the method that recognizes this is called "direct"—it doesn't rely on a process of becoming. This directness applies to the whole range of spiritual activities offered by the direct path.

We'll start with karma yoga. Karma yoga is usually considered to be the yoga of action, in which the fruits of one's actions are dedicated to the guru, to one's deity, to other beings, or to awareness itself. But Shri Atmananda has his own take on karma yoga!

Karma Yoga

About karma yoga, Shri Atmananda says:

> Of all these margas, *karma-yoga* alone has an advaitic goal called "naishkarmya-siddhi"—i.e. to be engaged in all the activities of body, senses and mind, and at the same time to be convinced beyond all doubt that you are neither the doer nor the enjoyer at any time, but only the ultimate witness or Truth itself.[46]

This approach to karma yoga is versatile. You can "perform" karma yoga in this sense at any time, with any activity. You can engage in volunteer work, social service, and social activism, as well as more mundane activities, such as fixing a leaking pipe in the kitchen. As you perform an activity, you can use the reminder (see below) that the doer and the recipient of the action are the same: "the ultimate witness or Truth itself." The opportunity to do this is always available to you.

Bhakti Yoga

The direct path allows for bhakti yoga ("devotion"), but there's not much emphasis on it in the works of Shri Atmananda. The bulk of his teaching on devotion is found in *Notes*. For Shri Atmananda, bhakti yoga should be directed toward the person of the guru, not toward a deity. Here's a representative passage from *Notes*.

> That particular person through whom one had the proud privilege of being enlightened, that is the *only* form which one may adore and do *puja* to, to one's heart's content, as the person of one's Guru. It is true that all is the Sat-guru, but *only* when the name and form disappear and not other-wise. Therefore, the true aspirant should beware of being deluded into any similar devotional advances towards any other form, be it of God or of man.[47]

Bhakti yoga usually involves adoration and doing *puja*, which includes invocations, prayers, and rituals. Even though Shri Atmananda was a fairly traditional Hindu teacher, he didn't recommend that aspirants begin worshipping traditional deities such as Shiva, Krishna, Durga, and Kali. His approach seems to be that if you feel that bhakti yoga should be part of your path, then the object of your devotion should be the guru. This was perhaps because of his emphasis on jnana yoga and the important role the guru plays in unfolding the truth for the aspirant.

Another topic that relates to the role of the guru is the teaching found in *Notes* that states that a living teacher is necessary for lib-eration. In his "Life Sketch" of Shri Atmananda, editor Nitya Tripta says, "He asserted most emphatically that no aspirant, however great, could ever attain liberation without the help of a Karana-guru in person."[48]

I should point out that Atmananda was emphasizing only that aspirants should hear teachings pertaining to the truth of their nature expounded in person from the guru, not that they should worship a guru bhakti-yoga style. I discussed this in chapter 4, "The Guru Doctrine."

Reminders

Reminders are short, simple, intense contemplations that don't involve inquiry. Shri Atmananda mentions quite a variety of reminders, which help you change your perspective by reducing your doubt and confusion. Experiencing the correct change of perspective is one of Shri Atmananda's definitions of liberation.

Here are examples of reminders given in the direct path. Notice that they don't all assume an absolute or final perspective. That's exactly why they can be helpful. They're designed to resonate with your perspective at particular points along the path and then shift your perspective toward a more holistic view.

- Remember that changes such as birth, growth, decay, and destruction are features of physical matter, which is an object of consciousness.

- Remember that words such as "consciousness," "knowledge," "being," and "happiness" all point to the "I."

- Remember that when you attribute physical reality to the world, you're also identifying consciousness with the body.

- Think about the true "I" indirectly, since you can't think about it directly. You can think of it as the residue left after everything objective has been removed from what we usually take to be the "I."

- Think of an object—for example, a coffee cup—in the same way. Remove all objective qualities from it, and all you have is the "thinking." But the "thinking" is also an object. When this is removed, what's left is your nature: witnessing awareness. Witnessing awareness is not an object but rather that to which objects appear.

- Contemplate how even the words "awareness," "consciousness," and "happiness" point only to the true "I."

- Keep in mind how your true nature is that into which all thoughts subside. If you follow any thought as it subsides, it'll take you to your true nature.

- Contemplate how the "I" is always the observer of experience, never the observed object.

- Ask yourself, *How, if there's no color without seeing, is it even possible to see a color?* This applies to all the sense objects, not just color. Do you have to believe it when your thoughts say that objects exist?

- Ask yourself, *How, if there's no color before seeing, and no color after seeing, can there be color during seeing?*

- Ponder this: Can a thought touch its object? Can it meet or make contact with the object in any way? If not, then how can the thought be "about" that object? How can it be "caused" by that object?

- Keep the great Advaitic aphorisms in mind: "Ayam atma brahma." ("This self is all there is.") "Tat tvam asi." ("You are that"—in the second person because it's told to the student by the teacher.) "Aham brahma 'smi." ("I am all there is.") Make sure that you interpret the words in their indicatory sense, not their literal sense. "You" and "I" refer to awareness. "That" refers to existence or "all there is."

- Contemplate the witness aspect of awareness. The deeper your contemplation, the quieter the mind becomes. This quietness, combined with contemplation, gives you the opportunity to experience the mind itself as witnessed.

- Contemplate "I am." This is not a state but a description of the truth of your being. This truth doesn't depend on being asserted, but the contemplation drives away all competing thoughts. Slowly the contemplation becomes deeper and deeper until happiness is experienced, which is the nature of the "I." At this point the "am" disappears, being no longer needed.

- Remember that spiritual or meditative states apply to the mind, not to witnessing awareness. Even the most subtle and profound *nirvikalpa samadhi*[49] is a state of mind that can come and go. The coming and going appear to you as witnessing awareness.

- Bear in mind that when you stand as awareness, perception and thinking vanish.

The reminders help you recapture specific key insights and stabilize on them. You can choose insights that are familiar but need more exploration. You can work with insights that feel challenging. And you can choose reminders that don't seem very clear but arouse a sense of mystery or wonder. And you can create your own reminders.

When you use one of these reminders, don't just repeat it to yourself. You're not trying to brainwash yourself or simply memorize the reminder. Instead, dig into it. Try to recapture the steps that led up to your insight. Or you can recapture the teacher's presentation, or your sense of wonder about it, as well as the insight itself.

Recapturing the insight will help counteract any doubt and confusion. It'll clarify that bit of the teaching. This clarity will radiate out and improve your understanding in general.

When you reach the point of realization or the aha moment, stabilize on it. Stay there and let it sink in. Try not to pursue another thought. Don't congratulate yourself. Don't even evaluate how you're doing. Just stay with that peak moment of insight. As you stabilize in that moment, the reminder will take you directly to the truth of your nature. You'll feel an opening into warmth. This peak moment will eventually become fainter and fainter. That doesn't mean it's leaving you. It's just returning to the silent witnessing awareness from which it came. As it goes, it'll take you with it. You'll experience a small homecoming.

Of course, sooner or later you'll turn to other things. Other thoughts and actions will arise. But for a moment, you'll have experienced being taken to the truth experientially with the help of one of these reminders.

In his various texts, Shri Atmananda recommends doing these reminders over and over again. They all remove uncertainty and take you experientially to witnessing awareness. And as any single reminder becomes clearer, they all become clearer to some extent.

Standing as Awareness

When you stand as awareness, you take the perspective of the transparent witness immediately. Your experience begins to verify this stand. This is a little different from reaching the witness through inquiry. With inquiry, you investigate what seems to be other than awareness, and through direct experience you realize that nothing is other than awareness.

But when you stand as awareness, the effect is immediate. It's as if you're stepping into the infinite right here. It's like saying to yourself: *I know that the teachings say that I am awareness. What if it were really true? Let me now take the perspective of awareness. The "I" is awareness, not a body or a mind. What follows from this? Appearances come and go, so they can't be me. As awareness, I don't suffer. I don't even have experiences—I am experience.*

Awareness doesn't do anything. It doesn't need anything. Nothing is missing. Awareness doesn't suffer. There might be unpleasant arisings, but they don't take hold. They don't last. They're simply witnessed as they come and go.

This isn't the perspective of the person. Even the person comes and goes in witnessing awareness, which is the truth of your nature. You're already this awareness. Taking a stand as awareness is just a way to be awareness a bit more knowingly.

When you take your stand like this, your experience will confirm the stand. This is similar to what happens in everyday life, in which your everyday experience seems to confirm your everyday stand. Your everyday perspective says that you're the body or the mind. Therefore, your experience seems to verify this perspective, and it seems as if things affect the body and the mind. From the everyday perspective, even this "taking a stand" business seems an exercise, something you're doing on purpose. It might seem like an artificial visualization.

But when you stand as awareness, you notice that things change. When you stand as awareness, what seemed to be true from your everyday perspective isn't even on your radar. What shows up is different, and what seems convincing is different. From the perspective of you as awareness, nothing happens to you. All "happenings," "bodies," and "minds" are themselves passing appearances. They're arisings in awareness, which is the single true "I."

If standing as awareness sounds appealing to you, keep the following points in mind.

First, it isn't a process of "fake it till you make it." If standing as awareness were really a put-on, then how could your heart feel the sweetness, peace, and contentment that it does when you're in the middle of that stand? Also, if standing as awareness were a process of faking it, then that would mean that you aren't really awareness after all. So then what would you be?

Second, taking a stand only seems artificial when you aren't taking your stand. That is, any artificiality or "doingness" is only from the everyday perspective of the person. But from the perspective of witnessing awareness, you never took a stand. You were always this witnessing awareness and have never departed from it at any time.

Third, standing in awareness becomes easier and more stable each time you do it. The in-between times are lighter and sweeter too. That is, those times when you're going to work or doing chores around the house will be lifted by the stand you took earlier. This is wonderful. The quality of your experience will improve even when you aren't explicitly taking your stand.

The Heart Opener

Whereas standing in awareness uses an explicit shift in perspective, the Heart Opener dramatizes falling in love with awareness.[50] You feel your way into the transparent witness.

It's very simple to do: After taking a deep breath or two, close your eyes. Sensations, feelings, thoughts, or sounds may arise. They arise against a clear, silent, and untroubled background. The silence is lucid clarity. Because this clarity isn't an appearing object, it can't be covered up by sensations, feelings, thoughts, or sounds. This clarity is witnessing awareness itself. Because witnessing awareness isn't perceived, it can't be said to be present or absent. It feels as if it's behind any appearance. Actually it's the source of appearances. Appearances arise against the backdrop of this silent, clear awareness and then peacefully subside back into it.

It's no mistake that your "I" notices this happening, because this witnessing awareness is the very nature of the "I." In your direct experience, the "I" is always there, whether appearances are present or not, whether they arise or subside. You're already there. Comings and goings—both appear to you as awareness.

This clarity has no edges. There are no borders or limits where the clarity stops and something else begins. You don't experience the clarity to be ten meters or ten miles in diameter. You don't observe it to have a color or shape. It's infinitely more subtle than that. If a color or shape arose, it would arise against this clarity, which is never not there. Because this openness allows for all appearances and doesn't block any of them, it's also known and experienced as unconditional love. You can feel this openness. This is the "heart" aspect of the Heart Opener.

This opening of the heart can't be owned. You can't hold on to this clarity (although you might want to, because it feels so good), because you already *are* this clarity. If a desire to hold on to this clarity happens, that desire isn't even "yours." It's just a temporary object arising against this same background of clarity that you are. The Heart Opener is a way to emphasize more directly the loving aspect of your nature as awareness.

The Heart Opener is also an antidote to feelings of nihilism. It counteracts despair and hopelessness. If doing self-inquiry hasn't provided you with a sense of sweetness, then the Heart Opener just might do the trick!

Sleeping Knowingly

"Sleeping knowingly" is the subject of Shri Atmananda's very first dialogue in *Notes*. In the direct path, sleeping knowingly is a way to realize that you're not an object and that you exist even when no objects are experienced. This teaching is an alternative to the usual Vedantic teachings on *nirvikalpa samadhi*, which teach the same two points. But unlike *nirvikalpa samadhi*, deep sleep requires no practice or cultivation. It's within the reach of every aspirant. As a method, sleeping knowingly is most helpful during the earlier parts of the path, when it still seems natural that you experience a waking state, a dream state, and a deep sleep state. (Further along the path, you deconstruct memory and the whole idea of "states." You see through the notion of time and memory.)

In deep sleep, you return to your true nature, which is objectless awareness. Deep sleep is defined as sleep with no emergent thoughts, appearance, or objects of any kind. Even the dream state is a case of awareness in which subtle objects arise. But during deep sleep, there are no objects at all. The way to sleep knowingly is to first keep this in mind as you relax and open into sleep.

Then, when you wake up from sleep, contemplate the fact that there was no object present during your deep sleep. Even though there were no objects in deep sleep, you don't feel as though you stopped existing—there seems to be a form of continuity between sleeping and waking from sleep. You acknowledge that you existed even though there were no objects arising. What can you be, in that case?

You're that to which objects appear. You're objectless awareness itself, which is present even when objects are absent. Not only were you not gone during deep sleep, you were also not suffering. *Ah, I slept happily!* This also confirms that you're the Love aspect of awareness.

In this way, you come to understand that you aren't an object and don't depend on objects in order to *be*. This is significant, because we usually think the other way around. We usually assume that the body is continuous throughout deep sleep, even if we don't continuously observe the body. We assume that the body is the carrier of our identity. But using the experiential approach of the direct path, you don't assume that the body is present when not experienced. You don't need to assume that, because you were there anyway—as awareness.

If the body isn't present in our experience, and yet we're not absent, this shows that we have no support for the normal assumption that the body is the locus of our identity, including during deep sleep.

In my own inquiry, I thought about this a great deal. I used to ponder:

> *Either my true nature continued unbroken during deep sleep, or it didn't.*
>
> *If my nature did continue, then it can't be anything observable, because there was nothing observable during deep sleep.*
>
> *If my nature didn't continue during deep sleep, then it stopped. Then, whatever woke up the next morning had a different identity, a different nature, than what went to sleep the night before. Why? Because there was nothing during deep sleep to keep this identity the same. It would be like dashed lines on the roadway; each is a different line from the others.*

But it never seemed that I had a different identity the next day. I never felt as if I had totally disappeared during deep sleep and become something new the next day. Therefore my identity couldn't have depended on anything observable. What was left? Consciousness with no objects.

"Sleeping knowingly" is a way to work with deep sleep itself to transform your experience. It transforms your sleep too! You'll find that going to sleep knowingly counteracts the associations that deep sleep usually has, such as negation, blankness, darkness, and slumber. All of your other inquiries will begin to expand. You'll feel more in touch with a permanent vastness, spaciousness, and lightness.

Guided Meditations

Guided meditations are usually narrated by the teacher. You'll find them less often in written material and more often done at retreats and other meetings with a teacher.

A guided meditation could be described as a visualization of some aspect of experience. As the listener, you follow the guide in a very open, relaxed, and loving way. The narrator takes you on a verbal journey involving some aspect of the mind, the body, or the world. By following closely, you forget your usual identification with the body or the mind, and you come to experience the objects and events in the narration as awareness and love. You experience openness and inseparability. Afterward, you can replay the meditation— either as a recording or, better yet, in your own mind. You can even create your own guided meditations. They all serve to make some aspect of experience more at home as awareness, as inseparable from you.

The Yoga of Awareness

Sometimes called Body Sensing or Subtle Body Yoga, this is one of the most helpful activities in the direct path. Quite often, if you attend a retreat given by or cultivate a teaching relationship with a teacher of the direct path, you'll be taught the Yoga of Awareness. You may be able to find Yoga of Awareness videos on the Internet, and you can find this yoga taught in the form of experiments in *The Direct Path: A User Guide*.[51]

The Yoga of Awareness is a wonderfully experiential way to deconstruct two common body-centered notions. One is that the physical body exists objectively, apart from awareness. The other is that you're the body. The Yoga of Awareness gives you experiential verification that neither of these notions is true.

To the casual observer, the Yoga of Awareness looks like low-impact, non-competitive hatha yoga. If you were to observe a session, you'd see people moving their heads, arms, shoulders, torsos, and legs very slowly, without emphasis on extreme postures or angles. You'd hear guidance from the instructor, but it would be different from most hatha yoga sessions. You'd hear loving guidance that invites the participants to experience the body and movements as awareness.

In the Yoga of Awareness, you don't experience the arms and legs as physical objects moving through space. You experience the body and its movements as spontaneous appearances in luminous global clarity. You don't experience yourself to be moving. Rather, you experience physicality and movement as flows of appearance to awareness.

This yoga transforms even your everyday experience of the body. You may find that it no longer seems that the body is "you" or contains "you." The body seems less and less like a heavy, opaque container for a non-corporeal self. It seems lighter and lighter, as if transparent, as if illuminated. The world lightens up too. The difference between you as awareness and the body, the chair, the table, or the floor begins to fade away. It's not that you're spacing out. It's more as if the world becomes your body.

I haven't found many non-dual teachings besides the direct path that work with the body in this way. In recent years, more and more non-dual teachings have begun to look for ways to "embody enlightenment" as a way to keep non-dual teachings from being too "heady" and from engaging only thoughts and feelings.

The direct path doesn't try to bypass the body, its sensations, its movements, or its concerns. The direct path includes the body. The Yoga of Awareness leads you to experience the body as awareness, as luminosity.

This yoga dissolves some of the most difficult stumbling blocks in the direct path, which are related to the everyday notion of the body and awareness as containers for experiences. The container metaphor seduces us into thinking that awareness is inside of the body and that experiences are inside of awareness. Some non-dual teachings don't free us from the container metaphor, since they proclaim "The awareness in you is the same as the awareness in me."

According to the direct path, awareness can't be "in" anything, because awareness isn't a physical object. Spatial relationships simply don't apply to awareness. Awareness has no limits. Anything that could serve as a border or container for awareness, such as a cranium, a bag of skin, or even a concept, is itself nothing other than an appearance that's witnessed by awareness.

The Yoga of Awareness provides powerful experiential help with understanding this. Since awareness isn't physical or spatial, then neither are the appearances that arise to be seen by it. These appearances include the body. With the Yoga of Awareness, you counteract any assumptions that the body *contains* awareness. You become able to experientially verify the body's nature *as awareness*.

I say more about enlightening the body in chapter 7, "The Opaque Witness."

CHAPTER 6

Witnessing Awareness— Introduction

In this chapter, I discuss the direct path's approach to the notion of witnessing awareness and how this notion is used in inquiry. In the direct path, witnessing awareness is the "I." It's defined as the "unseen seer": that to which appearances appear. The idea of the witness is intimately linked to the idea that appearances appear.

At the beginning of your direct-path inquiry, some qualities— such as memory, attention, preference, and free will—seem to be inherent functions of the witness. At this stage, the witness seems able to remember, to direct attention, and to prefer things. This kind of perspective about awareness is called the "opaque" or "lower" witness. As you continue the investigation, you come to examine these very functions. You realize that they're like colors and sounds—they appear as observed objects rather than functions built into the witness. Your ideas about the witness and about who you are become clarified. You don't build in so many attributes to the witness. When the witness starts to feel this way, the direct path calls it the "transparent" or "higher" witness.

Because the witness is a tool of inquiry and not a lasting meta-physical entity or attachment, it begins to dissolve when it has done its job. The process summarized above is discussed in more detail in the present chapter, as well as the following three chapters, which are about the opaque witness (chapter 7), the transparent witness (chapter 8), and the dissolution of the witness (chapter 9).

Direct Experience

The tool of witnessing awareness works hand in hand with the tool of direct experience. When direct experiences appear, what is it that they appear to? They appear to witnessing awareness. This is where the two tools work together. At the beginning of your inquiry, it may seem that appearances appear to the mind. This is the everyday view. But a little further along the direct path, you realize that the mind also appears. The mind isn't constant. Therefore, the mind must be appearing to something beyond itself. The mind can't appear to itself, just as a knife can't cut itself. That's where witnessing awareness comes in. When you realize that the mind appears to witnessing awareness, your understanding of yourself clarifies. It broadens, becoming more loving and less entangled in unwarranted assumptions.

How the Direct Path Sees Witnessing Awareness

The witness, sometimes called "witnessing awareness," is a teaching tool used in several spiritual paths. The idea of the witness derives from the Atman/Brahman idea in Advaita Vedanta, which is a time-tested, viable spiritual path. The witness idea leverages your preexisting intuitions about being a subjective center. It simplifies these intuitions so that you no longer seem separate from witnessed objects. You no longer seem different from other people, because you realize that the subjective center isn't a discrete and boundaried, concretized separate entity, so it's neither subjective nor objective. The purpose of the witness teaching is to help you experience that there's no separation or division or limitation in your nature.

According to the teachings of the direct path, witnessing awareness isn't a person or a mind. It's that to which these objects appear. It's also not the same as biological sentience or waking-state consciousness. Those functions come and go according to the state of the organism.

Witnessing awareness isn't the kind of thing that can come or go. Coming and going themselves are appearances that appear to witnessing awareness.

There aren't two or more witnessing awarenesses (see below). Witnessing awareness has no color, shape, size, location, or phenomenal characteristics. It has no psychological characteristics either. For these reasons, it isn't the kind of thing that can appear as an object. *Thoughts* of it can appear, but witnessing awareness can't appear or disappear. In a very minimalist way, you could think of witnessing awareness not as an entity, but as a sort of structural requirement that goes along with the very idea of appearance. If there seem to be appearances, then witnessing awareness is what they appear to. It's single and unbroken. If you witness one thing and then witness another thing, you feel as though they both appeared to the same awareness. You don't feel there are several witnessing awarenesses. As an observer, you feel that whatever appeared, appeared to you. Your own unity is the unity of witnessing awareness. But the "you" isn't a mind or a person.

Witnessing awareness isn't a gatekeeper. It doesn't filter appearances or decide which ones it will allow to arise. It allows *all* appearances, never saying no. For this reason, and because there's no suffering in awareness, awareness is often likened to unconditional love.

You may sometimes feel that there are objects or states that are beyond the witness or that there are somehow internal unwitnessed structures that make up the witness. It's natural to feel this way at first, because you start off thinking that awareness is the mind. And you're sure that there are objects outside of the mind. But if you have an intuition about a global clarity that unifies all things, you'll begin to see that this clarity is indeed awareness itself. In fact, as mentioned, the mind is one of the objects that appears to awareness. Whenever you've witnessed the mind change from active to sluggish to active, you've experienced the standpoint of witnessing awareness.

Unlike the mind, witnessing awareness is an unlimited perspective. It's a clarity infinitely more subtle than space. It's not made of vibrational energy, so it has no energetic limits. It's not physical, so it has no spatial borders. You never directly experience witnessing awareness to have any limitations at all. In your direct experience (which happens from the vantage point of witnessing awareness), you never know or perceive anything like an edge at which things stop. There's no border with unexperienced objects on the other side. You never experience the unexperienced. After a while, you stop being sure that there are objects outside of awareness. It feels as if the mind has limits but awareness has no limits.

When you look at experience and there no longer seems to be anything external (or internal) to witnessing awareness, witnessing awareness has finished its task as a teaching tool. Sooner or later it dissolves into happiness and contentment, with no sense of identity whatsoever. Not even "I am awareness." There's no sense of localization or individuation. As this stabilizes, the entire notion of the "witness" is no longer needed. Witnessing and appearing no longer seem to apply to experience. This is sometimes called the "collapse" of the witness, and it's equivalent to non-dual realization.

Why Use a Witness Idea in the First Place?

Why is the witness tool used, as opposed to some other tool? Many people don't resonate with the witness, and many paths don't use it. But many people *do* resonate with it. Many people have mystical or deeply intuitive experiences, even as children. When they encounter spiritual teachings, they find the idea of a global awareness that serves as the nature of the self and all things profoundly resonant. For people with these resonances, the idea of witnessing awareness as used in the direct path offers three main practical virtues.

One virtue is that the witness teaching tool is very intuitive. Even though the witness isn't a mind, it's similar to how we think of our everyday experience. In an everyday sense, "I" think things appear to "me." The witness teaching retains this overall idea about experience. It merely redefines what the appearances are appearing to. The result is a very simple and intuitive teaching.

Another virtue is that the witness teaching allows extremely subtle dualities to be examined and then dissolve. Dualities include classic opposites such as good/evil, right/wrong, popular/unpopular, love/hate, here/there, and us/them. More subtle dualities include self/other, mental/physical, and body/mind. Even more subtle and abstract dualities include truth/falsity, one/many, and subject/object. The witness teaching in the direct path has ways of seeing through all of these dualities. It's a very effective tool, one that's able to go "all the way" in this teaching.

The last virtue is that the witness teaching is "eco-friendly." By this I mean it's a teaching that cleans up after itself. It dissolves when no longer needed, and it leaves no lasting attachments to its tools and notions. This even includes the notion of awareness itself.

Some inquirers might think that these three points aren't virtues at all. The approach may sound too casual. An inquirer might say, "Well, if you're saying that witnessing awareness is just a tool after all and not a true reality, then why do I need it? Just show me what's really true. I don't need any tools in order to attain realization—many teachings say so."

Yes, there are teachings that advise you to avoid tools, inquiries, practices, and provisional teachings. They assert that *you* are the ultimate here and now and that nothing is required.

But notice the irony here. The very teachings directing you away from tools are themselves serving as tools. As tools, they're employed to have a performative effect on the listener. Most often, those tools attempt to hide their status as tools and masquerade as final truths, whereas the direct path's tools are transparent about their role as tools.

If you follow a spiritual teaching of some sort, you'll be using a tool. So you might as well try various tools and go with what works for you!

For me, the witness teaching fits the bill nicely. All three points about the witness teaching worked well for me in my investigations. I found the teaching to be intuitive, far-reaching, and ultimately able to collapse on its own when no longer needed. It fit nicely with

Western approaches I had devoted myself to earlier in life, including those of Brand Blanshard and George Berkeley.

How Many Witnesses Are There?

A typical non-dual answer to the "How many witnesses?" question is "one." This answer is practical. It gets the main message across, which is "not two or more." Hearing "one" helps prevent people from thinking "many." It helps lead them away from the easy assumption that awareness is the mind, and thus there must be as many awarenesses as there are minds. But "one" isn't literally or empirically true.

Awareness isn't an appearing object, so it's not countable. Awareness would be countable if by "awareness" we meant the mind, which tends to be separate from person to person and being to being. Awareness would be countable if it were something like smoke. A hotel could have a hundred rooms filled with smoke. There could even be many different kinds of smoke, depending on the nature of the materials being burned. But awareness isn't like this. It can't be broken up or compartmentalized by appearances. Because awareness, according to the direct path, isn't an object and isn't able to be broken up, it can't be a countable thing. Numbers don't make sense when applied to it.

Because numbers don't make sense when applied to awareness, it doesn't make sense to truly insist that there's exactly *one* awareness. Insisting on "one" awareness objectifies it and entails the logical possibility that there could be multiple awarenesses. But the non-multiplicity of awareness is more radical than this. It's not a matter of numbers.

So what can we say about the non-multiplicity of awareness? If I were to look at the direct path from a philosophical or spiritual perspective that was rhetorical, functional, or minimalist, I'd say that witnessing awareness is a kind of formal requirement that goes along with the language of appearances. That is, when we speak of appearances appearing, we need to supply something for them to appear to. Otherwise, they wouldn't be seen.

The more you have an intuitive feel for tapping into something larger than the visible world, the more you may resonate with the idea of awareness as used in the direct path.

When teachers of the direct path say non-dual-sounding things, such as "Awareness is the self," these slogans address intuitions about how appearances are structured. That is, when something appears, people feel that they're on the subject side rather than the object side of the event. The direct path merely gives the name of "awareness" to this subjectivity and expands on it.

More Than One?

The direct path differs from views that posit more than one awareness. For example, in our everyday way of speaking, we think of each person as having a separate awareness. This is because we think of awareness as coming from brain activity. There are many brains, so there must be many "awarenesses" (though we wouldn't pluralize this word in everyday life).

Another view that posits many awarenesses is the Geluk order of Tibetan Buddhism. According to this school, there are as many awarenesses as there are appearing objects.[52] This system of Buddhism posits sensory awarenesses, mental awarenesses, and yogic awarenesses. Each type of awareness is multiple, because there's one awareness per object, and there are many objects. In this type of Buddhism there's no notion of awareness that does the same work as the awareness concept in the direct path. The direct path is located in the Hindu tradition of Vedanta, and conceptualizes awareness differently.

Less Than One?

The direct path differs from types of inquiry that posit no awareness at all. For example, modern neuroscience would probably answer the "How many awarenesses?" question with "zero."[53] Some of this research tends to favor the reduction of mind to molecules and brain functions. The research implies that molecules and their pathways exist but that "mind" doesn't exist in the same way. The mind and its awareness are no more than epiphenomena of molecular activity. There's no other candidate for awareness in this branch of science. There's no universal or mystical awareness lying behind everything.

Of course neuroscience isn't intended as a spiritual path. But I know a number of people who practice an informal sort of metascience as a way to lend gravitas to the conceptuality behind their spiritual activities. If the mind is nothing other than molecules, then the "self" can't possibly be the mind. The notion that "I am the mind" is one of the most tenacious false ideas we have about ourselves. Because science can help free us from this false idea, it can be a powerful ally to self-inquiry.

One per Person?

The direct path also differs from spiritual paths (such as orthodox monotheism) that assert one soul or awareness per person. In the orthodox paths, God is said to be one, but the person's awareness or mind or soul isn't identified with God. The spiritual work is done not through that kind of non-dual insight but through more traditional spiritual means. Of course the orthodox paths have esoteric or hidden branches, which tend to accord a lot more closely with non-dual approaches. But if you enter monotheism by walking through the temple doors, you're likely to encounter the orthodox approach first.

So How Many Really?

Zero? One? More than one? Surely one of these must be correct!

I don't consider this issue to be a matter of fact or a matter of right or wrong. In my own experience with paths that disagree on these issues, I don't try to settle the disagreements metaphysically. I don't think of it as an empirical question, such as the number of eggs in a basket. That is, I don't ask, "How many awarenesses are there really—regardless of paths, concepts, models, or background assumptions? What's the objective truth of the matter?" I see no way that questions such as these can make any sense. It's not that I believe that there's a true answer out there. Rather, the question has assumed objective matters of fact that aren't verified by experience.

So I take a practical route. I don't assume a priori metaphysical certainties or universal answers that are supposed to apply beyond all possible concepts and conditions. I say: "Let's see what happens if I take this path. If I do what it says, will I go where it goes?" In the case of the direct path, my experience is that it works as advertised.

How Does the Witness Teaching Work?

The witness teaching looks closely at experience, showing you how to deconstruct dualistic perspectives. The witness teaching makes it clear that there's no evidence for distinctions such as self/other, observer/observed, here/there, one/many, and other fundamental dualisms.

The witness teaching moves from the gross to the subtle. Beginning with the "outer world," it allows you to discover that there's no physical object experienced apart from color, sound, texture, flavor, aroma, or other sensations. Then you discover that there's no sensation without the appropriate sensory modality, such as seeing, hearing, or touching. Then you discover that there's no evidence of seeing or hearing independent of witnessing awareness. The only common and stable factor is witnessing awareness. Nothing is ever experienced to be present other than witnessing awareness.

You may often hear that "There are no objects." Taken by itself, this phrase can be misleading. It implies that in your inquiry you may find stuff missing. But that's not how it goes. You don't look everywhere inside of awareness and everywhere outside of awareness and come back to report that all objects are absent where you expected them to be present. You don't discover nothingness in place of an object that happens to be absent.

What you discover is much more radical. You find that the entire experiential structure that assumes objects exist is simply not verified by direct experience. There no longer seems to be a place for objects or absences of objects. You find no stage setting decorated with objects, no missing objects, and no seats to hold a separate observer. You find no "there." The entire setup becomes dismantled into loving clarity and peace. Earlier in your path, objects and your observation of them may have felt like necessary parts of your experience. But through your investigation, all this is pacified.

But Maybe the World Really Does Exist

Many inquirers get an idea about the direct path that causes them concern. The idea is that the direct path looks all around and concludes that the world doesn't exist. This concern arises because of how the direct path differs from most people's everyday perspective: the perspective in which the world is said to truly exist in an objective way. When this objectivist perspective is challenged, it can be scary.

Even at the beginning of the direct path, this perspective is investigated, and it isn't always a comfortable process. When you do direct-path inquiries, you can begin to feel as if you're missing a great big world out there. It can feel as though you're denying reality. You may think:

> What about the stuff outside of awareness? Maybe the world really exists as it seems to, but we're unable to verify it in an objective way. Maybe we're brains in vats. Maybe we're computer simulations in a real, extraterrestrial world, and our experience is just programmed to look as it does. Maybe all this non-dual inquiry isn't able to really give us any true certainty about the world.

So rather than saying that there's no world independent of awareness, isn't it better to say that we just can't be sure? We can't be sure one way or another whether there's a world out there. Isn't this a more modest, humble, and accurate way to state how things are?

This concern is common for most people who investigate deeply. It's a concern derived from the realist account of experience, in which our personal experience is said to be caused by objectively real objects impinging upon the sensory membranes of the organism. According to the realist everyday account, things in the world are real. They already exist whether they're perceived or not. The organism may or may not come into contact with things. It may or may not receive sensations from them. But the objects exist all the same. An unperceived object is no less real than a perceived object. The difference is only whether the organism has come into contact with it.

In realism, the organism's contact with an object sets up a chain of causation. The cause begins in the object and the surrounding conditions. The effect is the organism's experience. Sometimes the experience is said to "correspond" to the object, as when an experience of water is caused by water. Sometimes the experience is said not to correspond to the object, as in cases of illusions. For example, a mirage in the desert looks like water, but it's really just an effect of light rays, heat, refraction, sand, and perhaps wishful thinking on the part of the observer.

The realist account is designed to hold up even in the case of illusions. That is, regardless of whether experience is said to correspond to objective reality or not, the overall causal chain is similar: something outside of the organism's experience is said to cause the organism's experience.

The skeptical view of realism is that we just can't know for sure whether there's a world. This feels like a safer statement, one that's less likely to be proved incorrect. Notice two interesting things about the skeptic's approach. First, it doesn't support realism. It's actually a challenge to the realist's account of causation. The realist is claiming that experience is caused in a certain way. The skeptic is saying that we can't know whether this is true. The realist is unable to answer the skeptic. The realist tendency to cite more and more causal chains won't convince the skeptic that the realist account is truly accurate. Second, even though this type of "we can't be sure" skepticism isn't intended to support realism, it does so nevertheless.[54] Even though the skeptic doesn't accept any particular realist account about experience, the skeptic accepts a causal account in general. The skeptic seems to be saying that something must be objectively true—we just can't be sure what. We can't be skeptical in this sense unless we have an underlying belief endorsing realism.

But the direct path's approach is so radically different from realism that even the skeptic's cautionary statements say too much. The direct path isn't offering a competing causal account of experience. The direct path doesn't seek to show *how* experience happens. The direct path doesn't assume that objects exist either inside or outside of experience.

In fact, one of the subtleties of the direct path is that it doesn't conceptualize experience as having an inside or outside. It doesn't use spatial metaphors to describe experience or awareness.

To think of experience as having an inside or outside is to regard experience as if it were a physical object. It makes experience analogous to a very large shopping bag. In everyday terms, a shopping bag can have objects inside of it and outside of it. Objects can move from the inside to the outside and from the outside to the inside. But to think of experience in this way is to commit a *category mistake*. Making a category mistake is defined as attributing a property to something that couldn't possibly have that property—for example, attributing free will to brain tissue or thinking that green ideas sleep furiously. Attributing physical properties to witnessing awareness (including the properties of location and containment) is a prime case of a category mistake. It's a case of being seduced by the container metaphor of experience.

The direct path doesn't physicalize or localize experience. Instead, the direct path explores the reality of experience, looking into its nature and ramifications. The exploration never ends up verifying duality or separation. Nothing turns up missing. The exploration leads instead to the discovery of wholeness, intimacy, immediacy, sweetness, and joy.

Witnessing awareness, which is another term for experience, isn't conceptualized as an object, a container, a place, or a state. It's not thought of as an illuminated region or an exalted energy throughout space. It has no spatial or phenomenal qualities. It doesn't decide or remember anything. It performs no actions or functions. It isn't a cause. Its characterizations tend to be minimalist, such as being "*that to which appearances appear*." Shri Atmananda calls it the "I-principle." To the extent that you can come to see the "I" as a principle, you are freed from the idea that the "I" is the body or the mind. Seeing the "I" as a principle is a lighter, freer and more open way to think of yourself. It also reduces the impulse you may have to visualize awareness as something physical. And as your inquiry proceeds, there comes a point at which you don't even think about it anymore!

This is the approach taken in the direct path. The direct path isn't making another set of realist claims. It's not offering a story to compete with scientific theories of reality. So even the skeptic's warning doesn't apply to the direct path. You don't even have to discard the scientific account. If you're a scientist or psychological researcher, and you take up direct path–style investigation, what you'll discover is a wide-open freedom in which these two approaches don't compete with each other. You'll discover that the direct path's joyful irony and freedom from competition serve to keep the approaches out of each other's way. There's no conflict. You might even begin to be more creative!

What's Direct About Direct Experience?

The direct path leverages our everyday distinction between "direct experience" and "indirect experience." These categories aren't flawless or airtight. They end up dissolving with inquiry further along the path, but the distinction is used because it can be helpful in inquiry.

Ordinarily we think that (a) some experiences—for example, the appearance of color, sound, or pain—happen with no interpretation, inference, or conclusion making and (b) other experiences—experiences that we can articulate using sentences, such as "I see an orange"—require some sort of conceptual processing, either conscious or subconscious, usually involving a claim about what's happening or what something is.

Examples of direct experience might be articulated as "red here now" or "loud" or "ouch." Because direct experience doesn't depend on inference and usually doesn't include a claim about what causes the experience, these aren't the kinds of things that can be either true or false. They're more like momentary impressions than statements.

Examples of indirect experience go further and often contain some sort of existential claim about what's responsible for the experience, such as (a) "That's a red ball," (b) "I heard a car crash," or (c) "I stubbed my left toe." Because of the inferential element, statements articulating indirect experience can be mistaken. For example, statement (a) could be false because the ball was really white under red lighting. It *appeared* red, but it *wasn't* a red ball. Statement (b) could be false because the sound heard wasn't from an actual car crash—it was only a recording. Statement (c) could be false because it was a case of phantom limb pain. Perhaps you lost your left foot while you were in the military. But you can still have a pain-in-the-left-toe feeling.

Indirect experience is usually based on at least some direct experience. And the same direct experience is compatible with more than one indirect experience. For example, the same red appearance can be the basis of an indirect experience of a red ball or an indirect experience of a white ball illuminated by red light.

In the direct path, direct experience is investigated very closely. The overall questions guiding the use of direct experience are these: Does direct experience establish a separate self, an objective world, and a sense of separation and suffering? Or does direct experience establish wholeness, clarity, and love?

When people begin studying the direct path, they usually think that experience justifies their ideas of a separate self and an objective world. So the direct path has students look very closely at these ideas to see whether they're verified by direct experience. Students begin by looking deeply into the experience appropriate to each sense. What's directly experienced in vision? In hearing? In the sense of touch? After examining the objects of the senses, students look into the body and then the mind. They look at the whole category of "inner" or "non-physical" types of experience, such as emotion, thought, memory, and reference.

What they discover in each case is that no separation or distance or objectivity is verified by direct experience. They discover an abiding presence, clarity, wholeness, and sweetness. They're freed from the inferential elaborations that claim that people are separate, limited, and alone.

This abiding presence carries the wonderful fragrance of loving-sweetness beyond conditions. The sweetness doesn't come from pleasant appearances; it's the very source of appearance. It can't be blocked, shut off, or overturned by any appearance. It's already there, as the very nature of everything that arises. And when the last dualities cease, it no longer makes sense to speak in terms of arising or appearance. All is sweetness, clarity, light.

Direct experience isn't operative forever. It's a useful teaching tool only because it's an intuitive idea people normally already have before they begin studying the direct path. The direct path simply expands on the idea and uses it as a tool of investigation. The tool fades away as the whole idea of appearance fades away.

In fact, sooner or later in the direct path, all concepts fade away. Good examples are the divisions between types of experiences, such as "sensation," "feeling," and "thought." But these distinctions help you get going with your inquiry. They're helpful during the beginning and middle stages of the path. Further along the path, you investigate and ultimately deconstruct them.

An Example of Non-dual Inquiry: Looking at an Orange

Normally, it seems as if there are countless objects in existence; it seems that we observe some of them, while many others go unobserved. We think that objects cause our perceptions of them. For most people, this is more than a scientific theory; they think experience is really and truly like this. This is the perspective of "realism," a perspective that students of the direct path discover isn't supported in any way. In our direct experience, there are no objects either present or absent. Experience and awareness are the same thing, often called "warmth," "sweetness," or "love."

Direct-path inquiry doesn't tackle all the supposed objects at the same time. Instead, it begins with the objects that seem more obvious and easy to isolate. In other words, inquiry proceeds from gross objects to subtle objects. It begins with the world and then continues with the body, the mind, and other subtle objects.

In every case, the result of the investigation is surprising, even momentarily shocking. But ultimately it's heartwarming, exhilarating, and simple. You don't experience "otherness." You don't experience "sameness." You don't experience existent objects. You don't experience non-existent objects. You don't experience objects in awareness. You don't experience objects beyond awareness. What you experience is nothing other than presence itself, openhearted clarity, and limitless love.

In the direct path, you investigate your experience by breaking it down into sensory modalities, examining one sense at a time. It may seem that this approach assumes that the breakdown of experience into senses[55] is a given truth. What if experience is really unbroken, and the division into senses is just a contingent artifact of our biology? Aren't we just being arbitrary? You'll investigate this very point later. Early on in your investigation, however, looking at your experience sense by sense is a basic and intuitive way to proceed. Later, you'll find that it doesn't matter too much anyway.

You'll see again and again that regardless of how we categorize experience, we never verify the presence of an object the way we often think we do.

Let's take an example. Because vision is the easiest sense to talk about and think about for purposes of illustration, imagine that we're looking at an orange. So, if we go by visual experience alone, what evidence for the orange's existence is directly available? The discovery happens in stages. In our direct experience:

- **There's no orange apart from an orange color.** That is, apart from an appearing orange color, we don't experience an orange-colored round physical object.

- **There's no orange color apart from the notion of seeing.** That is, apart from the idea of seeing, we don't experience something existent in front of us called "an orange color."

- **There's no seeing apart from witnessing awareness.** That is, apart from witnessing awareness, we don't experience an independently existing sensory modality called "seeing" that happens to be out there sending us information. What's present is awareness. It's present as "presence," not a present "thing." And presence is never not present.

In a nutshell, in our visual experience, there's no orange apart from the color, no color apart from seeing, and no seeing apart from witnessing awareness. The only thing that's verified and constant throughout is witnessing awareness. And witnessing awareness isn't an object.

These three insights are some of the most radical and transformational insights in the entirety of the direct path. Even though they come early in your investigation, insights similar to these are verified over and over, no matter what you investigate. In a manner of speaking, if these realizations are sufficiently generalized, the rest is quite easy. These insights contain the entirety of the direct path.

Let's take these insights one at a time.

No Orange Apart from an Orange Color

It may seem that there's really an orange out there causing us to have experiences of the orange. But this is just what we'll investigate in our direct experience.

An orange color appears. How does our visual experience verify that it's caused by a real orange? How does our visual experience affirm that it's not a photo, a hallucination, or a 3-D chalk drawing on the sidewalk? Our visual experience of these things could be identical.

More important than the question of illusion, holograms, and trompe l'oeil is this: in vision, no matter how much we see, we don't have visual experience of a color belonging to a preexisting object. Even if we saw the orange cut up into pieces with various other colors appearing, our vision wouldn't be able to distinguish between *color* and *a colored object*. Vision has no notion of "physical objects," which have many attributes, including color. Vision deals with colors alone. Vision can't distinguish between

a. "orange color" and

b. "an external physical object to which the orange color belongs."

That distinction is conceptual, not visual. Therefore, to believe that the color *belongs* to the orange or that the orange *has* this color is to believe a concept. It isn't our direct experience. Our direct visual experience simply doesn't make claims about what's there, what's causing our experience, or what something is.

So in our direct experience, there's no evidence of an orange apart from an orange color. Of course we can generalize this to other colors, other objects, and other sensory modalities.

The following statement is one of the powerful lessons of direct experience in this experiment. If there were really an objective orange out there causing our "orangely" color experience, then direct experience should be able to provide evidence of it. But it doesn't. Direct experience is a supremely close-focus attempt to look at what's going on. But it never provides any support for the idea that things are really "out there" sending information to "me, in here." Instead, what *is* supported is our experience as awareness.

Using witnessing awareness together with direct experience, we discover experientially that there's no separation and that experience has always been "direct."

No Orange Color Apart from the Notion of Seeing

This is the same sort of discovery at a deeper level. Maybe there's no evidence of an orange actually being there. *But surely*, you may think, *the color is there. Isn't it? How can it be seen if it's not really there?*

Even if you believe that the brain causes experience (a claim investigated by the direct path), at first the orange color really seems to be there in your experience. So even if you start off as a materialist, you need to look into the evidence for the existence of color in your direct experience. Ask yourself:

- *What's my direct experience of this color?*

- *Do I experience the color as some kind of thing that's really there, existing before me?*

- *Do I think of the color itself along the same lines as a colored object?*

When we see a colored object, we normally think of it as having existed outside of our field of vision before entering our field of vision. Is this also how we think of the color?

In everyday terms, we may think of an object such as a tennis ball as being able to enter and leave our visual field. We seem to be able to verify that the tennis ball has left our visual field because we can no longer see it, but, for example, we can still feel it. We seem to be able to keep track of its existence through other sensory modalities.

But this kind of interpretation can't apply to *color* itself. We can't touch color. So how can we verify that a color has left our visual field? Where has it gone? We can't verify that it went somewhere else after it stopped appearing to us. It's not that we aren't sharp enough to keep up with this color. It's rather that we're making a category mistake in thinking of color in this way. Going by visual evidence in our direct experience alone, we have no way of justifying a claim that the color is still present. It just doesn't make sense to think of the color as something that exists when it's not seen.

If it doesn't make sense to think of the color as existing unseen, then it doesn't make sense to think of it as existing when it *is* seen. This kind of interpretation is fine in the everyday sense, when we're trying to find our cat in the house. "I know she's here. I hear her. I just can't see her!" But with color, in our direct experience, this makes no sense.

Guided by direct experience, if it makes no sense to think of the color as existing either seen or unseen, then it doesn't make sense to think of it as existing in the first place. It makes no sense to think of an existing or a non-existing color. If we go by direct experience, then not even memory, inference, or the testimony of others can help establish the objective existence of color.

Instead, what makes sense in terms of direct-path investigation is to think of "color" as another word for "vision." That is, it's not that we "see" colors that are there to be seen. It's more that the seeming appearance of color is what we mean by "seeing."

No Seeing Apart from Witnessing Awareness

So, then, what about seeing? This is the same insight, one step closer to awareness.

Does seeing exist as a process on its own? Is it an independent sensory modality? Other than the appearance of color, which isn't experienced as an independent object, just what evidence do we have for "seeing" as an independent process or perceptual object, as something existing on its own? In what way is it separate from the "seer" or from awareness?

Well, "seeing" certainly isn't a sense object. It's not the physical eyes. It's a sensory function. You can't see it or hear it or touch it. You might have a belief that says that "seeing" truly exists. But that's merely a claim. What evidence do we have for the existence of "seeing"? And whenever "seeing" seems to be present, witnessing awareness is *already* present as that to which "seeing" appears. Seeing is just another object appearing to witnessing awareness. Whenever seeing arises, witnessing awareness was already the case.

You might argue: "You don't see witnessing awareness either. So why do you give it a pass? Why do you think that witnessing awareness exists?"

This is an important point. As I discussed earlier in this chapter, witnessing awareness isn't an entity or an object or a state. The direct path isn't saying that witnessing awareness "exists" or "appears." Awareness is not the kind of thing that could exist or not exist. Awareness is just that to which appearances appear. It's the unconditional love that allows all things.

This has been an example of an experiment that begins with an object that seems to be part of the objective physical world. Through very close examination, in which we leave aside inference and assumption as much as possible, we end up affirming nothing other than awareness. This doesn't mean that the world doesn't exist, because a non-existent world makes as little sense as an existent world. In either case, we would have to have affirmed a world before we could apply "exists" or "doesn't exist" to it. None of that is established by our investigation.

Conclusion

In the direct path, witnessing awareness is taught as that which is appeared to. This teaching doesn't appeal to everyone, but many people find it powerful and helpful. The teaching of witnessing awareness begins by inviting you to focus on your everyday experience, providing a way for you to look into the unexamined assumptions that make you feel separate.

Over time, as your examination continues, witnessing awareness will seem less and less like a separate entity inside you (that is, it'll seem less like a mind). It'll feel more and more like a global, clear spaciousness. The world, the body, and the mind will feel less and less separate and cut off from one another. As you investigate, you'll discover that whatever seemed to be separate is the "self" of awareness only. As the "realist" gestalt of separate objects weakens, the sense of witnessing awareness dissipates as well.

CHAPTER 7

The Opaque Witness

The direct path makes a loose and informal distinction between types of witness. Types of witness differ in how embedded the witness seems to be with psychological functions. There's what I call the "opaque" witness (also called the "lower" or "thick" witness). And then there's what I call the "transparent" witness (also known as the "higher" or "thin" witness).

The opaque witness is a sort of anthropomorphized witness: witnessing awareness when it seems to have built-in psychological characteristics or other properties. The opaque witness is like a giant mind. If you hear non-dual teachers answer "Why are we here?" questions by saying "Awareness *is* itself but desires to *know* itself experientially," that kind of awareness is what the direct path would call the opaque witness.

The transparent witness comes later in the process of investigation: witnessing awareness when it's free of properties other than being appeared to. Any psychological properties, such as desires, goals, or subconscious areas, are not properties *of* the witness but merely appearances *to* the witness. They're spontaneously arising appearances analogous to colors and sounds. Just as the witness has no colors, it has no desires.

You'll notice that I say "seems to have." It's not that either type of witness is truly "out there" as a true layer or level of consciousness. They aren't forms of experience waiting to be properly discovered. If the direct path is a form of pedagogy, then the witness is a teaching tool. It's an explanatory perspective or an experiential gestalt.

In this way of looking at the witness, its seeming characteristics are an effect of the direct path itself. As a tool of investigation, witnessing awareness seems to change as you progress with inquiry. Early on in the path, when you're investigating the world of gross physical objects, the witness naturally seems grosser, thicker, more opaque. But later, when you've discovered the physical to be nothing other than awareness, the next step is to investigate the subtle world of mental objects. At this point, it's natural that the witness seems more subtle as well.

From Gross to Subtle

I'll explain more about the difference between these types of witness. But first I'd like to discuss why the direct path's investigation goes from gross to subtle. Why doesn't it go the other way around, from subtle to gross?

Besides the fact that Shri Atmananda presents the *tattvopade-sha*[56] in this order, there are several practical reasons. One is that at the beginning of your inquiry, grosser objects—such as chairs, tables, apples, oranges, sidewalks, buildings, and bridges—are easier to focus on. They seem so obviously to exist separate and apart from you, apart from witnessing awareness. As a beginner, you can more easily keep your attention on these objects. They don't require as much concentration. Later on, with more investigative experience under your belt, it's easier to do the parallel investigation on more subtle objects, such as thoughts, feelings, desires, concepts, and mental states. They don't seem as slippery or insubstantial as they would have if you had begun your inquiry with them.

Another reason to go from the gross to the subtle is that we often think of subtle objects in physicalist terms. So if you deconstruct physical objects first, you're ahead of the game.

We commonly think of the mind as some sort of bucket-like container. We think of memories or thoughts or words as if they are physical objects residing inside containers. So if you're able to see that it's never your experience that physicality is real or objective, then physicalist metaphors for mental objects lose a lot of their power to seem literal. The very idea of containment is a concept, and a concept can't contain anything. A sensation can't contain anything. If you realize this very clearly before you investigate the mind, then you can apply this insight to the mind as well. You'll then be less apt to visualize the mind as a bucket. You'll be less likely to think of memory as a container of hidden objects. Your realization that the mind doesn't contain dark spaces will be that much more powerful. You won't be misguided as a result of taking metaphors literally.

The third reason to go from the gross to the subtle is that doing so prevents the investigation from prematurely deconstructing its own tools. The tools of investigation, such as visualization, inference, and "higher reasoning,"[57] are themselves subtle. You don't want to investigate them too soon and make them unavailable before they've completed their job. Their time will come.

Occasionally you may wish to take a shortcut, deconstructing the mind or even the witness, and then be done with the path. "Why wait? Let's get to the end now." But if you deconstruct witnessing awareness too soon, it may lose its utilitarian, transformational power. It may no longer make sense as a tool. Then you may not feel motivated to use it in investigation. In such cases, you may have realized that a thought is merely an appearance, but you may still feel anguish when you're physically separated from a loved one. Having deconstructed your main tool, you won't be able to inquire into brute physicality. Physicality is at the root of the concepts of separation and alienation.

But if you do the investigation from gross to subtle, then the various kinds of suffering related to physicality and its metaphors are impossible. There'll be no "place" where you as awareness aren't present. "You" as awareness are never separate from anything. The order of investigation makes a remarkable difference in practice.

How the Opaque Witness Comes About

The opaque witness comes about indirectly. Your inquiry begins with the world of physical objects. The more subtle types of experiences, which include mental phenomena, aren't looked into. You don't investigate the witness. You don't investigate the process of investigation. They aren't excluded; they just come later.

During the early stages, it's natural to regard these subtle phenomena as part of the internal wiring of witnessing awareness. After all, you hear a lot about witnessing awareness, and you think about it. And from everything you're already familiar with, what is it that most seems to resemble witnessing awareness? The mind. So it's quite natural to think of witnessing awareness as being like a big mind. And since the mind is said to have desires, memories, and intentions, it's easy to attribute these things to awareness. There's no need to clarify these issues during the early stages, when you're concentrating on physicality and embodiment. The issue of mind versus awareness gets clarified later.

In fact, the opaque witness is a natural by-product of the process of investigation. And it's all you need in order to see that the physical world and the body aren't independent from witnessing awareness. If the teaching insisted on using only a clarified, transparent witness at the beginning of the path, it would be too abstract to work with.

If you continue with the investigation, the witness will be clarified. Most intermediate to advanced students encounter one particular sticking point that forces the issue, that being the issue of multiple sources of awareness. The question arises: "I can see my thoughts. Why can't I see yours? If I am awareness, I should be able to see all thoughts, not just the ones that happen in *this* body."

Sublation

The multiple-awarenesses question is a good example of how, in the direct path, witnessing awareness becomes less opaque. There seems to be some tension between the feeling of awareness being personal ("I can't see your thoughts") and a person-based interpretation of the official teaching ("Awareness is supposed to be able to see everything, and I am awareness, aren't I?").

This tension sets up an energizing crisis point analogous to a Zen koan. In order to dissolve this tension, the direct path encourages students to reexamine the very same model of witnessing awareness that worked so well earlier on. The same insights and concepts that helped to deconstruct tables and chairs won't work to deconstruct multiple points of view. You need sharper tools. With a skillful mentor, the result is often an aha moment. In the case of the multiple-awarenesses question, students usually come to discover that they were attributing physicality or localization to witnessing awareness. After this discovery, they're forced to adjust the model toward greater subtlety. For example, their newer, lighter model of awareness might be that physicality and localization don't ever divide or localize awareness in the first place. Instead, physicality and localization are only arisings appearing to placeless, non-localized awareness. This is a significant discovery that broadens the field, making the witness seem more subtle and transparent and less like an individual mind.

These kinds of shake-ups and insights, called "sublations" by philosophers, happen at several points along the direct path. Sooner or later, students of the direct path reach a sort of crisis point that makes them question certain aspects of the teaching itself. They resolve the tension by discarding the cruder version of the spiritual teaching, or at least the part that had puzzled them. They adopt a more sophisticated version of the teaching, one that accounts for the puzzling issue that caused the crisis. They may even take the new model as a final truth. Of course the new model will itself fall away at some point through investigation, even if it doesn't seem like it at the time. At the time, the discovery feels new, exciting, and even sort of permanent. This provides motivation to continue the inquiry.

When beginning students hear about this process, they often say, "Well, why not skip intermediate steps and take me to the final truth right away!" This is the point at which some paths often reply with cryptic statements such as the following:

- "You couldn't take such strong medicine."

- "The truth would be blinding."

- "You are that."

- "The seeker is the sought."

- "There's nothing to do."

- "All there is, is pure consciousness, which is *you*."

- "The final model is no-model."

But these days, of course, most non-dual students have already heard most of these high-level, oracular pronouncements. In the age of the Internet, these pronouncements have lost their power to shock. They've become memorized slogans. At the same time, they don't give us much to work with. People still need advice on how to intrepret these sayings in a helpful way. So if students are sincere in their desire to come to the end of their search, they usually come back around to engage with a "lower" level of teaching anyway. It has more traction while still offering challenge and inspiration.

This is how the witness becomes more transparent in the direct path: through sublation.

The Body

The body is like other physical objects. But it's very special too. It's a physical object that, when touched, seems to send you its own signals. If someone else touches a table, you see him or her touch the table, but you don't feel anything. If someone touches your arm, you see it, and you feel something too. Not to mention, if someone touches your arm in a certain way, you feel pain. The body seems real. The events of movement and touching, the feelings of "being touched," and the very existence of a painful feeling add to the reality effect that the body has.

And you may think of other bodies as similar to yours. Because you think, *I feel it when the experimenter touches me,* you may also think, *You feel it when the experimenter touches you.* You may seem to know this by analogy.

If you can see how the orange is nothing but awareness but still think of the body in these terms, then this is a case of your experiential gestalt being that of the opaque witness.

Because the body is more experientially complicated than a table, the direct path has you investigate the body only after you investigate other physical objects. That way, by the time you get to the body, physicality doesn't seem like a pivotal issue, and the body doesn't seem as if it truly exists in a physical way. After all, when you realize that the world and all its objects aren't physical, how could the body be the only exception? How could the body be the only physical object in a world full of arisings to awareness?

By the time your investigation reaches the subject of the body, it's the "special" aspects that need attention, not the supposed existence of the body as physical.

How Does the Direct Path Investigate the Body?

It's extremely helpful for you, as a student of the direct path, to do the various kinds of movement and Yoga of Awareness exercises described in *The Direct Path: A User Guide.* These exercises provide a supportive, inspirational context in which you can discover the body to arise as sensation-like appearances to awareness. In this sense, the body is perfectly analogous to a table or a chair. This discovery is an aha moment.

The more complicated fact that the body seems to be the center of feeling and perception is no exception. Sensations, perceptions, and feelings are easy to understand as arisings to witnessing awareness. More complicated body-centric notions, such as the following, are also arisings appearing to awareness.

- *Ugh. That pain is being felt right there in the arm of this body.*

- *That itch is being felt here and not over there.*

- *The body that feels that contraction is the same body in which I feel trapped.*

- *If this pain were really awareness, I'd be able to get rid of it by thinking about something else. Therefore it's really real on its own.*

To a great extent, the specialness of the body as compared to other objects arises as a thought. And of course thoughts are also arisings appearing to awareness. Even the notion that thoughts, feelings, and sensations are naturally distinct from each other is something that the direct path investigates.

Casually speaking, we could attribute the power of the thoughts-versus-feelings idea to the way we're commonly educated. In school, anatomy, physiology, and perhaps psychology are taught as true, accurate, authoritative, and privileged ways to interpret experience. The popular scientific perspective is a complete 180 from the direct path's approach to experience. It has come to seem objectively true, as if written into the universe itself.

In the direct path, you investigate all these different cases of seeming truth and objectivity, finding in every case that they're nothing more than appearances arising to witnessing awareness. And later, you discover that they aren't truly even arisings. Even pain, which tends to seem so real, isn't directly experienced as pain or as independent from awareness. The same goes for pain's supposed causes. The discovery is analogous across the board—nothing is directly experienced to exist apart from awareness, which, according to the direct path, is your very self.

Because the direct path takes a non-metaphysical, nonreferential approach to language, these discoveries don't force you to abandon everyday talk and action. You don't need to give up your job or stop going to the dentist. To abandon these things would be to fall into a mix of absolutism and nihilism.

For example, you'd be falling into absolutism if you became so convinced about direct-path speech being the "truest" speech that you forced it upon your orthopedist or accountant. You'd be "absolutely" denying value to vocabularies other than the one used by the direct path. And at the very same time, you'd be erring toward nihilism. You'd be taking a nihilistic approach toward the non-direct-path vocabularies, seeing them as valueless.

The direct path avoids these traps. According to the direct path's generous non-metaphysical take on language (see chapter 3), there can be an engineer's vocabulary, a dentist's vocabulary, and a "body is only an arising" vocabulary. They can stay out of each other's way. There's no need to award one of these vocabularies a metaphysical privilege over the others and thereby quit working or avoid health professionals.

As you more thoroughly investigate the body, the senses of localization and contraction and embodiment diminish accordingly. Gross or subtle, what you seem to see is what you seem to be. Objects of all kinds become lighter and more subtle. Witnessing awareness becomes less and less opaque. Whatever "I" is seems to loosen up. It doesn't seem as tightly confined to the contour of a body. Many kinds of yoga, sports, music, art, cinema, literature, and dance help you feel expanded beyond what seems to be the periphery of the body. If the self were truly just the body, could these expansive experiences even be possible in the first place? What's wonderful about these various activities is that even afterward, the feeling of expansion remains. If you go dancing, you may feel light and expansive for days. The sense of localization may return, but perhaps it never shrinks back down to the same close limits it had before. The feeling of expansion afforded by so-called non-spiritual activities is a wonderful sample of the direct path's insight that there's no physical localization in the first place. If you can get a looser sense of localization even through cycling or through playing video games, it seems like confirmation that the direct path isn't making outlandish claims—it's really onto something!

In investigation, the body and its functions are the same as tables and chairs, colors and sounds. They arise and subside in witnessing awareness.

Bodily Enlightenment

The direct path is a teaching of bodily enlightenment. One of the main ways that the opaque witness begins to feel more subtle is through investigation into the body. The body receives a substantial part of the direct path's investigative attention.

In recent years, commentators on non-dual teachings have become more and more interested in the body. I regard this as a healthy corrective to the way that so many non-dual teachings focus on non-somatic issues such as beliefs, emotions, and philosophical abstractions. The body is left out of the picture. It becomes an inconvenience, perhaps a source of puritanical shame. Of course the common non-dual position is that nothing has separate existence. But sometimes, when people claim non-dual realization for themselves, they reserve a special, elevated category of non-existence for the body. This of course merely serves to underscore the unavoidable sense of existence it still retains for them. Perhaps inspired by tales of famous sages ignoring doctors when ill, students of nondualism define the body out of existence and then ignore its dynamics, movements, and concerns. The result is usually a severe lack of comfort and integration with respect to the body.

Recently, people have shown interest in correcting this. In an article called "Embodied Nonduality," Judith Blackstone discusses the importance of inhabiting the body in an integrated way, saying that "inhabiting the body reveals both an internal coherence and the subtle nondual transparency that pervades self and other as a unity."[58] Blackstone responded to an online comment with the following observation.

I have seen so many people express that they are "directly knowing" when they seem to be only open from the "neck up." [They] are knowing what's out there, but they have not realized themselves as the transparency.[59]

Scott Kiloby's observations are similar. In his article "Conscious Embodiment," he proposes that non-dual realization must include the body, not just the head.

I have no idea what people are talking about when they talk about awakening without the conscious embodiment aspect. I can only imagine that they are talking about a head awakening, where there is a sense of space or headlessness. I couldn't settle for that. My body wouldn't let me. It was screaming to wake up too.[60]

In the direct path, you examine the body in great detail, with loving intimacy. *The Direct Path: A User Guide* includes almost fifty pages of inquiry and exercises relating to the body. Direct-path retreats usually include a focus on the body. They feature guided meditations, yoga movements, and body-sensing exercises that provide the direct experience that the body is nothing other than awareness itself. The exercises may include stillness, movement, a sense of effort, and even some degree of resistance and discomfort as limbs and torsos extend in new ways.

In all these activities, the body is lovingly embraced and discovered to be inseparable from witnessing awareness. Not only does this help you make friends with the body, but it lightens the body, relieves tension, improves balance and mobility, heightens flexibility and posture, and opens up the opportunities for many body-centered activities that seemed unlikely or impossible. In my own case, these insights helped dismantle the illusion I had harbored about physicality being truly existent. I attained the courage and ability as an adult to learn inline skating and fixed-gear bike riding—both with no brakes. One can enjoy both of these with some degree of danger and caution on the streets of New York City (where I live). I attained better balance, wider peripheral vision, and new ways of understanding my surroundings. Others have been inspired to take up dancing, music, hiking, and other activities that they hadn't considered earlier.

The direct-path teachings on the body give you a sense of intimacy and integration. The less the body and the world seem like existing objects, the more closely and lovingly you'll flow with the body and the world.

Solipsism and the Question of Others

If you investigate with great depth and sincerity, you may reach a point where it begins to feel as if you're alone in a world of awareness and arisings. After all, awareness is "I," and what appears is said to appear to the "I-principle." In addition, you may hear non-dual slogans such as "There are no others" and "You are nothing other than my very self" and think:

- Are *there others? Am I all there is? This is getting scary.*

- *But what about my loved ones? I don't want to be in a world where they don't exist.*

- *If I am awareness and I can see* my *thoughts, then why can't I see* your *thoughts?*

I've noticed in my own inquiry, as well as from long experience helping others, that the confusion arises when key concepts are personalized. For example, when I say "I," am I referring to Greg? Or am I referring to witnessing awareness? Do I think that witnessing awareness is inside of Greg? Or have I realized that Greg is an arising appearing to witnessing awareness?

You can come to see how you're personalizing these questions by clarifying your terms. The adjective "other" has no meaning unless it applies to some sort of noun or substantive. It needs further specification in order to do its job of modifying, specifying, or distinguishing. You can ask, "Are there other *whats?*" In the present context, there are two main interpretations of "other": (a) other people and (b) other awarenesses.

Are there other *people?* Yes, in the everyday way of talking. It's obvious in the everyday sense. If there is "this" person, then there are certainly "other" people. The same thing applies to apples and oranges, tables and chairs. There's "this" one and many others. No non-dual path that I know of teaches that you're truly the only person there is.

Are there other *awarenesses?* If we interpret "awareness" as in the direct path, then "I" is awareness, and there can't be others. There's nothing that could slice awareness up into separate parts. An appearance can't divide that to which it appears. As discussed in chapter 6, "Witnessing Awareness—Introduction," there's no multiplicity of awarenesses taught in the direct path. So the answer is a straightforward no.

So far, so good. But this is just theoretical, at least until you inquire deeply into the world and the body. The more deeply you do these inquiries, the less it'll seem that there's anything apart from awareness. It won't seem that awareness is inside people. It simply won't occur to you to ask the question "Are there others?"

But when the "are there others" sticking point arises for students of the direct path, it's actually good news in several ways. One, it means that the teaching has taken deep root. Casual investigators usually won't feel any tension around this issue. Two, for those who resonate with the idea of global awareness as the nature of all things, the direct path has well-documented ways to get past this point.

The third benefit is that getting stuck here may help certain students realize that they don't fully resonate with the idea of global awareness—maybe they didn't really resonate with the guiding vision of the direct path in the first place. This realization will motivate them to find different approaches, approaches that they resonate with more deeply. And there are plenty of approaches that don't involve the idea of global awareness.

For some students, the direct path's teaching that awareness is global and not personal might not hit home until their investigation reaches this sticking point. When they discover that awareness doesn't come from the person—awareness is bigger and more fundamental than the person, and the person appears to awareness—they might realize, *Oh, so* that *is what the direct path means by awareness! Well, then, I'm not so interested.*

The End of the Opaque Witness

Even though the opaque witness is opaque, it's transparent enough to do its job. It doesn't need to be fully transparent in order to help us see that the world and the body don't exist as independent objects. For example, Bishop George Berkeley (1685–1753) retained the notion of individual minds and nevertheless accomplished a thorough deconstruction of the world and the body,[61] showing how to experience the world and the body as ideas only, not as physical objects.

The witness gets less opaque as you transition from investigating the body to investigating the mind. The witness still seems to possess free will, attention, memory, and desire, because it's being understood as a type of big mind. But when you investigate the mind, you look into these same phenomena. You'll soon discover them to be appearances and not built-in properties of witnessing awareness. After these discoveries, the witness will seem more and more transparent.

CHAPTER 8

The Transparent Witness

In this chapter, I discuss issues and problems surrounding the idea of the transparent witness. I cover how the direct path goes about addressing these issues. I discuss how the transparent witness leads to its own dissolution.

The direct path has certain self-canceling features that come into play quite prominently when the transparent witness is the main tool used. Ironically, the more work the transparent witness does in helping with your inquiry, the less of a "something" the witness seems to you. When it has done everything it can, it no longer seems like anything.

At some point in your investigation, three things will come together. One, nothing will seem truly physical anymore. Space, size, shape, position, localization, and movement will no longer seem to be objective phenomena. There'll be no more impression of physical separation. If these kinds of things seem to arise at all, they'll seem like ideas or notions, not true or external pieces of objective reality.

Two, you'll feel no puzzlement about the existence of "others." You won't wonder about not being able to see others' thoughts. It'll no longer seem that thoughts are phenomena generated by physical beings. You won't think that you're a separate physical body among others. It won't seem that you have an imbalanced access to thoughts—the kind of imbalance where you can see the thoughts somehow localized around your own person but not those localized around other people. The end of this puzzlement will be mostly due to your no longer being convinced by the physicalist model of things.

Three, your investigation will turn to the mind. In fact, the realm of the mind is so compelling that some students of the direct path wish to begin and end their investigation in this arena alone. This investigation confronts the mind (whatever you take it to be), as well as mental objects, activities, states, functions, and other subtle phenomena.[62] You'll look into the existence of sensation versus perception versus emotion versus intuition. These subtle phenomena, such as desires, beliefs, and choice, can seem just as obviously objective as sticks and stones. And it can seem that your identity is lodged there somewhere. Belief in the objectivity of these phenomena can cause a strong sense of separation, even though you don't believe them to be physical.

Once these three aspects of your investigation are in place, witnessing awareness will have lost a lot of the opacity it seemed to have earlier. In fact, the witness will become clearer more quickly than ever, since most of your investigation of the mind will tackle the very same things that you had considered mechanisms internal to awareness.

As I've mentioned before, the direct path proceeds from gross to subtle. Investigation into the world and the body will reveal that your nature isn't based on anything physical. Because you'll still feel a sense of individual identity, you'll naturally assume it resides somewhere in the mind. At this point in your investigation, witnessing awareness and the mind may seem one and the same. Investigation into the mind will clarify this. It'll show that the mind arises as an appearance to awareness and that there's no phenomenon that constitutes identity.

Just what are mental phenomena? There are so many ways to describe mental activities and objects that there isn't enough room in this book to include them all. But for most investigators, several mental features emerge as the most problematic. These functions tend to have the strongest reality effect as the bearers of personal identity. They include attention, emotion, memory, choice, authorship, belief, and desire. In my own investigation, I remember thinking: *It seems as though I'm the one who directs attention. It seems as though I'm the one who feels, remembers, chooses, performs, believes, and desires.*

For different investigators, different functions feel more compelling. In my own case, I spent a year investigating the choosing function. I'd been asking, "Is this where my identity lies?" It turns out that "lies" was the perfect word, since investigation revealed that choosing wasn't truly my identity.

Example: Is "Attention" Who I Am?

Let's take a closer look at attention as an example of how the direct path investigates a mental function. Attention is a good example because it's more subtle than memory, choice, and desire, which you may already be accustomed to investigating. Attention has a way of seeming deeper and more intimately connected with who we are. It seems to be built more deeply into the witness. Even when other functions, such as choice and belief, are being investigated, it still seems that attention is operating behind the scenes, directing witnessing awareness to look at one thing and then another.

It may feel as if through attention, you can change what awareness looks at; you can change its direction, intensity, and breadth of scope. You may even visualize awareness as a light that illuminates objects, conceiving of attention as your way of controlling this light. Notice that this way of thinking is based on physical metaphors, such as direction, intensity, breadth, and scope.

Notice also that the metaphor of light encourages you to think of objects as preexistent—as being in the darkness of inattention until illuminated by the light of attention. Whether illuminated or not, the objects will still seem to be present, even if they aren't physical. Of course if you're no longer convinced that the world is physical, you'll be much less likely to take these metaphors literally.

So how do we investigate attention?

To take a specific case, let's say you're meditating. In this particular meditation, the instructions tell you to keep your attention on the breath—not on any memory, not on any feeling in the body, and not on any thought or mental image. If you notice your attention going to anything other than the breath, you just gently bring your attention back to the breath and try to keep it there.

Normally, you seem to have the ability to move your attention in several different directions. You can direct your attention to the breath, to a memory, to a cramp in your leg, or to your dinner plans. It seems that attention is something you can control.

You can investigate this understanding of attention as follows.

- Ask yourself, *Do I directly experience control of the attention, or is the feeling of control a spontaneous arising that appears to awareness, perhaps followed by a feeling of "I did that"?* Also, notice how often your attention seems to slip. This can help you more clearly experience it as a spontaneous arising and not something that you actually control.

- Ask yourself, *Do I directly experience a memory to be present when my attention isn't on it?*

- Ask yourself, *Do I directly experience a memory to be present when my attention is on it?* In other words, aside from what we're calling "attention," what's the direct evidence for a memory that's actually present?

Let's look at the scenario more closely. Something happens, which is given a standard explanation: *I'm meditating. Then a movie memory appears. Then I exert control over the attention and bring it back to the meditation.*

What just happened? You can look at every aspect of the standard explanation—the meditation, the control, the memories, and the movement of attention. Is the standard explanation really true? Is there an observed faculty of attention that belongs to awareness? If it really operates as you think, do you have direct experiential evidence for attention being an independent, operative function? Is it in awareness or witnessed by awareness? Or is it a mere appearance to awareness? Is the standard explanation itself just an arising that appears to awareness?

You can get closer yet. Ask yourself:

- *What's my direct experience of this situation?*

- *Is there any direct experience that these objects and movements are present, either outside of my attention or inside of it? Are these various phenomena directly experienced to be anything more than arisings appearing to witnessing awareness?*

- *Does awareness actually change direction, or is "awareness changed direction" a belief that arose spontaneously?*

For example, in terms of arisings, an example from your meditation could be explained as follows:

- Moment 1: A "meditation" appearance arises.

- Moment 2: A memory-arising appears: *I love Humphrey Bogart in that movie.*

- Moment 3: A decision-arising appears: *Let's get back to the meditation.*

- Moment 4: A feeling-arising appears: *Okay, moving back to the meditation now.*

- Moment 5: A conclusion-arising appears: *Here I am, back at the meditation, where I'm supposed to be.*

- Moment 6: A judgment-arising appears: *Hey, that last thought also strayed from the meditation.*

- Moment 7: A resolution-arising appears: *I better get back to the meditation and stay there.*

- Moment 8: A feeling-arising appears: *Okay, moving back to the meditation now.*

- Moment 9: A "meditation" appearance arises.

If you see this movement of attention as a series of arisings, you make an important discovery. You discover that attention, control, memory, and movement are not internal *features of* witnessing awareness but arisings that *appear to* witnessing awareness. What seemed like an internal function that perhaps housed your individual identity is nothing more than a temporary appearance.

You discover that in your direct experience there are neither hidden, unilluminated objects of attention nor presently illuminated objects.

You discover that witnessing awareness doesn't move or choose or focus attention. Witnessing awareness is unmoving and unchanging. Even attention itself is just another object. Verbally, it's nothing more than a word people use to refer to one particular arising among others.

As with the World, so with the Mind

Just as witnessing awareness doesn't have the quality of being red or blue, it doesn't have the quality of illuminating things or controlling the direction of attention. It has no phenomenal characteristics whatsoever. This becomes clearer and clearer the more you investigate the various phenomena of the mind.

This investigation turns out to be quite similar to your investigation into the world and the body. In each case, you discover that in your direct experience there's no evidence of an object actually being present (or absent). All that's present (as presence) is witnessing awareness itself.

Non-dual Sticking Points and Traps

As your inquiry into mental phenomena continues, witnessing awareness becomes more and more transparent. Various functions and structures that had made witnessing awareness seem mind-like, you discover, are only passing arisings. You don't experience any borders or limitations at all to witnessing awareness itself.

The investigations below use the notion of arisings. This isn't to claim that arisings really and truly arise. Rather, the ideas of witnessing awareness and its arisings are used to look into phenomena that seem real and independent of awareness. When it no longer seems that there's anything other than arisings, then there'll no longer seem to be arisings either. This is discussed further in chapter 9, "Non-dual Realization and the End of the Witness."

However, for some investigators, the usual inquiry doesn't resolve certain issues. These issues seem sticky and stubborn. I call them non-dual "sticking points." Myself, I had two of them—free will and the subject/object distinction. These issues are usually related to well-ingrained metaphysical ideas that have a stronger than average reality effect for people. The particular issues may differ from one person to the next, but the reality effect can be so strong that it calls the entire path into question. For a student who's at a sticking point, it may seem preferable to abandon the direct path altogether than to try to see through his or her metaphysical notions. Below I'll outline some of the most common sticking points, along with the direct path's keys to their dissolution.

The Non-existence of Other People

One potential sticking point is the idea that other people don't exist. You can get this idea if you misinterpret the direct-path investigations. If you interpret global awareness as biological sentience or the personal mind, then the direct-path investigations may give you the idea that you're alone in the universe. I've known a few people over the years who've had this reaction when pursuing the teachings on their own.

But when awareness is interpreted as global, not as the mind or anything personal, then this issue tends not to arise.

Speaking as someone who writes about direct-path investigation, I can tell you that I haven't written an experiment that focuses on other people. Why not? Because I think of public media as a transmitter of non-dual pedagogy. I think about how the reader can use a book or a video to consume non-dual messages in any order. What if you encountered the investigation into people before the investigations into the world and the body? If you're doing the contemplations and investigations on your own, without the guidance of a teacher, it can get scary if the topic of investigation is other people. I've known people who have experienced nihilistic, solipsistic, and depressive reactions when doing non-dual inquiries on their own. These unpleasant feelings can arise not only when studying the direct path but also in conjunction with other non-dual approaches. So in my own writings, I've chosen not to go into much detail about the status of persons. I've also placed a lot of emphasis on doing the Heart Opener before doing the various self-inquiry experiments. The Heart Opener makes the mind more subtle, which can lead to more fruitful inquiry. In the context of inquiry, the Heart Opener also functions as a convenient antidote to feelings of solitude and hopelessness.

Teachers of the direct path seem to be in agreement about this. I notice that books and videos about the direct path don't feature investigations into the status of "other people."[63]

You see others as you see yourself. So if you truly don't see *yourself* as a person, a body, or a mind, then you won't see *another* as a person, a body, or a mind either. You won't feel alone, because you'll be confident that your nature is the nature of all things. Your heart will open. You won't feel cut off. You'll have the warm and loving feeling that by your being awareness, everything is included and nothing is missing or denied. In my own case, direct-path investigations never caused me loneliness, alienation, or nihilism. Quite the contrary. Everything and all people came to feel as close as my heart, because all are of the same nature.

The Inability to See Other People's Thoughts

This stumbling block is similar to the question of whether there are others, discussed above. But this one has a special concern. It's related to a belief that, as awareness, one ought to be able to see the thoughts of others.

This belief comes from a confusion between awareness and the mind. Non-dualism says that there's only one awareness, that all arisings are appearances to this one awareness, and that awareness is what we really are. *Therefore*, you may think, *I should be able to see any thoughts that arise anywhere. But I clearly can't see anyone else's thoughts, so there must be something wrong with non-dualism.*

Notice that "thoughts" and "others" make sense if we're talking about minds, but not if we're talking about awareness as described by the direct path.

This sticking point may come up most strongly while you're investigating the mind, because it's in that phase of the investigation that you move from seeing awareness as a mind to seeing awareness as the global clarity to which minds appear.

The feeling that you ought to be able to see others' thoughts is based on some sticky assumptions:

a. That which sees thoughts is individual and belongs to a person.

b. There can be many of these seers.

c. That which is seen belongs to a person.

d. There are many of these objects (including persons and thoughts) available to be seen.

These assumptions were most forcefully articulated by the seventeenth-century dualist philosopher René Descartes, who characterized the mind as an indivisible, non-physical thinking thing inside the body—one mind per person. As a thinking thing, according to Descartes, the mind is able to know itself. It knows that *it* exists, but it's prone to error when it tries to know anything else. In order to be sure about anything beyond our own mind, Descartes said, we need God's help.

The concerns articulated by this stumbling are straight out of Descartes. Most students of non-dualism retain these assumptions even years into the non-dual path. Some non-dual teachings don't even try to deconstruct these Cartesian assumptions.

The direct path deconstructs these assumptions in several ways. First, there's the down-to-earth reply: if non-dual realization allowed the realizer to see others' thoughts, then Shri Atmananda and other famous role models would have been virtually omniscient. But there's no evidence of this whatsoever. So maybe omniscience isn't such a sensible assumption to make. Maybe the assumption is off track.

Recall two of the dualistic assumptions involved in the belief that as awareness, you should be able to see other people's thoughts:

a. That which sees thoughts is individual and belongs to a person.

b. There can be many of these seers.

These assumptions are based on the idea that the body contains the mind and the mind is what thoughts appear to. But in direct-path inquiry, you understand that awareness has no borders or edges, and awareness can't be divided up on a one-per-person basis. You realize that the mind isn't what appearances appear to, because the mind is itself an arising that appears to awareness. You realize that the mind is an appearance and that appearances can't see anything.

There's a deeper realization as well. You don't even see "your own" thoughts! You're not a person or a mind. As awareness, you're not one of many minds. There's simply no basis in your direct experience for dividing appearance into "mine" versus "others'" or "here" versus "there." With this realization, the question of seeing "others' thoughts" simply can't arise.

The direct path has plenty of contemplations and experiments that allow you to realize that the body doesn't enclose itself around awareness and that the mind isn't the seer. As with many direct path–related issues, the most important discovery to make early on is that physicality isn't objectively existent. Therefore it can't function as a border or container. Also, because awareness is defined as "that which is appeared to," it isn't physical and can't be compartmentalized or divided up. These discoveries make inquiry into the body and the mind much more natural and intuitive. The fruits of these discoveries include blissful freedom and openhearted love.

Objectifying Enlightenment

Another sticking point involves objectifying enlightenment. This happens when you see enlightenment as a property of a personal entity (or a "non-entity"). In such cases, you regard both the property and the (non)entity as existent objects. They seem to exist in a real way. Real enough, at least, so that you take enlightenment seriously and literally, either feeling inferior because you think you lack it or feeling superior because you think you have it.

Objectifying enlightenment can turn into a trap when you take these ideas personally, as though they apply individually to you. You may have a deep feeling that you're not enlightened. You may regard a non-duality teacher as possessing a quality that you feel you lack. Then you'll want that quality for yourself. You might even suffer because you believe you lack a quality essential to happiness that others enjoy. This will throw you off the path, because you'll be concentrating more on attaining a personal status than on contemplating the nature of reality.

If you believe that you *are* enlightened, this can be even more of a trap. You'll feel "done." You might not be open to deepening your understanding. And of course, feeling as though you're enlightened represents a misunderstanding, a personal contraction, and a sense of separation. You'll feel distinguished from others. You'll feel elevated. You'll take yourself seriously, as if you have a special connection to a profound truth, whereas other people have farther to go. These feelings and beliefs will cut you off from the possibility of realizing that everything is always-already free from entification and free from possession.

The direct path avoids the issue of treating enlightenment as something objective. This is because the direct path isn't about a personal entity possessing a particular quality. There's no such goal in the direct path. The direct path doesn't personalize accomplishments. In fact, the very notions of "entity" and "quality" are inquired into and realized as nothing more than arisings—which is to say, awareness.

Even though the direct path doesn't personalize spiritual attainment, it doesn't object if you do the occasional "quality assurance" check to see whether your spiritual path is working for you. During these "QA checks," you can revert back to a comfortable, everyday, non-spiritual vocabulary. *Am I happier? More loving? More peaceful? Less confused?* Personalization is a part of this vocabulary. If you feel that your path is making you unhappy, anxious, contracted, or selfish, then you should reassess your path. There's no reason not to do these occasional sanity checks. But progress probably won't be noticeable from minute to minute, day to day, or week to week. Give it more time.

In direct-path terms, none of this is a personal matter. Of course it usually starts out feeling like a personal matter, which is natural. This is because at the beginning of the path, your view about everything is personal. The direct path takes this beginning gestalt into account and works with it knowingly. As inquiry and other direct-path pursuits proceed, the gestalt opens up toward the non-personal clarity of awareness itself. For many years, I've noticed a very deep irony about the whole issue of non-dual investigation. This irony applies to many non-dual paths, not just the direct path. That is, for those doing investigations, the less they think about personal attainment, the closer they are to non-dual realization. (And of course that sentence personalizes the process way too much.)

Cause and Effect

Even if you're comfortable with the direct path's teaching that objects can be deconstructed into "arisings," you may want to know the cause of these arisings. Does witnessing awareness cause an arising to appear? Does one arising cause another? Does an arising cause itself? How can an arising have no cause whatsoever?

The direct path approaches these questions by looking very closely to see whether there's ever direct experience of a cause. Imagine the following arisings:

1. A memory-arising appears: an insult you received last week.

2. A feeling-arising appears: an unpleasant sense of indignation.

3. A belief-arising appears: *(1) caused (2).*

Arising 3 asserts a causal claim. What would make it a true claim? How would that work? Is there a hidden relation between arisings? Is there some sort of process that manipulates arisings behind the scenes? Because you can't see this process, you may feel alienated because you can't put your finger on the exact mechanism. This may seem to make you feel worse than you felt already after you remembered the insult, in (2)!

The investigation looks very closely at these arisings. In your direct experience, do you have any evidence of a cause happening between (1) and (2)? That is, even if (1) preceded (2), does that mean that (1) *caused* (2)? Where's the direct evidence? That's what we're looking for to substantiate the idea of "cause."

Maybe awareness itself caused (2). Is there any evidence of this? How does awareness cause an arising? Is it like a hand pushing flowers up from under the soil? Is there another arising coming between awareness and (2) that helped give birth to (2)? And even if there were, what makes that arising the cause of (2) rather than a preceding arising? Okay, then maybe (2) causes itself. Is there any evidence of (2) causing (2) to happen? Would that even make sense? Because if (2) were there to cause itself, it would already be present. And if it were present, then what was the cause of *that* arising? This could lead to a hopeless infinite regression.

But actually, no cause whatsoever is evident in your direct experience. When you realize this, cause and effect lose their grip on you as sticking points.

Investigating cause and effect provides an "extra added bonus," as they say in the world of sales. It helps you deconstruct the idea of personal doership, which is its own sticking point for many people. After all, doership is a particular case of causality, in which you regard a person as the cause and a decision as the effect. According to do something is to cause it to happen. So if you realize that we never find cause or effect in our direct experience, then you usually realize that we can never find doership in our direct experience either.

Doership

Doership is a familiar issue to most investigators on non-dual paths. In fact some paths devote most of their teachings to this issue. In my own investigations, I contemplated doership for about a year. I was contemplating whether my true identity resided in the choosing function. I had already "seen through" a wide variety of other candidates for identity, and doership was the last holdout on my horizon. I really thought that my identity lay in being the chooser of alternatives and the doer of actions.

The direct path's approach asks you to find the doer you think is there. So you look for a doer-entity in your direct experience. Can you find a doer anywhere? Yes, there are thoughts that propose doership and claim it, too. For me, there are feelings of pride and anguish at a job "I" did well or poorly. There are contractions in my chest and forehead when "I" am criticized for an action that "I" claim to have done.

But thoughts, feelings, and sensations are not a true doer. In fact, when you investigate them, you realize they are nothing more than spontaneous arisings appearing to witnessing awareness. Direct experience verifies that no thought can be a cause or an effect of another thought, since each one arises spontaneously and causelessly from witnessing awareness, the same as any other arising.

So where would a doer be? This is what the investigation asks you to find in your direct experience. When you realize that no doer or chooser is found, the seeming reality of doership dissolves. It's no longer a sticking point.

Memory

Memory is formally similar to causality. It's another case in which we normally feel that there's an unseen relationship between arisings.

Let's take a close look at memory, as we did with causality. We can do this even without deconstructing time itself, which is more subtle and not often a sticking point. And after we deconstruct memory, the passage of time will seem a lot less real. Events won't so strongly seem to be truly happening in an objective way.

So let's say that there are two arisings, a past insult-arising (1) and a present memory-arising (2).

(1) The insult-arising that appeared last week

(2) The memory-arising that seems to refer to (1)

The direct path approaches memory by asking what makes (2) veridical. Let's examine the relationship between (2) and (1). What makes (1) a true event? What proves that the event mentioned in (2) actually happened? What's the link between (1) and (2) that verifies memory?

When (1) appeared, (2) hadn't yet appeared. And when (2) appears, (1) is no longer around. How can they be related? How can the supposed referential relationship between them be verified? The two arisings are never present together. They don't touch each other. They don't contain each other. Maybe the mind takes care of it. How would that happen? You may think that there's a subconscious area of the mind where all this is kept straight. But what's our direct evidence of such a region? What's our direct evidence of a relationship between (1) and (2) residing in this region? Yes, there are belief-arisings that make claims about these kinds of mental structures. But aside from these belief-arisings, what's our direct evidence?

When you deeply realize that there's no direct justification for any of these beliefs about memory, the feeling of the reality of the past and present loses much of its reality effect. You feel a wonderful sense of freedom. And you don't forget how to go to the store or pay your taxes! Those actions are also arisings that appear spontaneously to awareness. They need no extra managerial help from another arising!

The Coherence of the World

When so much of the physical, somatic, and mental world is brought under investigation, you might feel rebellious, as if too much is being deconstructed. You might want to admit that there's something real after all that makes the world seem sensible. The world really seems coherent, and that ought to count for something! You might feel as if continuing on direct-path inquiry might bring on madness. So you ask: "Okay then, so why do arisings arise in just this way? Why don't they seem totally random? Why don't things seem like a case of 'blooming, buzzing confusion,' as psychologist William James once quipped?"

These are frequent and valid questions. This issue of coherence can be a sticking point for people who feel that the direct path is asking them to give it up. These people might rather reject the direct path than reject the very obvious coherence they seem to experience. The coherence question is similar to the classic question "Why is there *something* rather than *nothing*?" Sometimes nondual teachers answer these questions with anthropomorphic statements, such as "Awareness wanted to know itself experientially." But in the direct path, by the time someone is looking into mental phenomena, it's too late for that kind of answer. It's too late to take seriously an answer that attributes desires to awareness. This kind of answer personalizes awareness, making it seem too much like an individual mind.

There are two ways the direct path approaches this question. One approach looks into the assumptions embedded in the question. A major assumption is that there really is a causal mechanism underlying the world that explains the way things look in general. Is this assumption warranted?

Let's assume for a moment that there really is such a mechanism. In that case, there are two possibilities. One possibility is that the causal mechanism is *part of* the world. In this case, the mechanism is incapable of explaining the totality of the world because it's unable to explain itself as a part of the whole. The workings of this mechanism itself would need further explanation. But there are no more tools to work with. So the workings of the world are ultimately left unexplained.

The other possibility is that the causal mechanism is *not part of* the world. In this case, where would it be, and how would it be able to act on the world? If it's supposedly in awareness, then you'd need to verify this object's presence in awareness the same way you've been trying to verify the presence of other things in awareness, such as choice, desire, and other functions (and your search to verify the presence of those functions always failed).

To verify the causal mechanism that makes the world seem coherent, you would need to find it existing either "in" awareness or "outside of" awareness. Can you find it in either region? Or is it nothing more than an arising that appears *to* awareness?

The other approach to the question "Why do things look coherent?" is taken quite often by Shri Atmananda in *Atma Darshan* and *Notes*. Western philosophers call it the *reductio ad absurdum* (reduction to absurdity) approach. In this approach, you take the question seriously and see what follows. It turns out that the question can't be answered. In order to answer the question, you would have to be able to make a type of comparison between two worlds that's impossible in practice and in theory, too. So the question ends up making no sense. It doesn't play fair.

Let's see how this works. First, let's assume that we really know that the world looks coherent. Why, then, does it look coherent rather than incoherent?

At first this question seems reasonable. It seems similar to other questions that ask about how things look: "Why is your shirt blue

After Awareness

and not white?" "Why did you get your hair cut so short?" "Why are the leaves brown on this tree?" In each case, we're able to experience both alternatives and come up with an answer explaining what we currently see.

But in the case of the appearance of the entire world taken at once, we can't do this. We can't survey global coherence on one side and global incoherence on the other side and then compare them and come up with a mechanism that explains coherence. Why not? Because if there were global incoherence, we wouldn't know it. If there were no predictability or regularity, it wouldn't seem like it. It wouldn't seem like anything at all. There needs to be some degree of coherence in order for incoherence to appear. In a globally incoherent world, the thought *Hey, this is an incoherent world!* wouldn't arise. The very observation, which depends on coherence, could never be formed in the first place.

Once you go into the question in either of the ways detailed above, the question loses its punch. You lose the sense that it really deserves an answer. You lose the sense that the progress of your inquiry depends on a true genealogy of the world. And you can get back to inquiry!

Wanting to See Awareness

This can be a sticking point because the direct path's main tool, witnessing awareness, isn't something that appears to the senses. The direct path asks you to verify everything through direct experience, but witnessing awareness itself can't be seen, heard, touched, or apprehended as any kind of object. This can be frustrating.

It's quite natural to want to put your finger on awareness and prove that it's really there. Therefore, many students demand to *see* awareness.

The direct path has a few ways to address this demand. One is by seeing indirectly, through expansion exercises such as the Heart Opener, which I recommend in *The Direct Path: A User Guide*. The Heart Opener asks you to slow down and to not try to observe anything in particular. It asks you to notice that (a) regardless of what arises or what doesn't arise, witnessing awareness is already present in order for arisings to happen in the first place. Witnessing awareness is present, not as an object that could have been absent, but as a sweet, clear stillness and openness. Also, (b) this witnessing awareness is itself noticed not as an arising but as something fundamentally more intimate than that, as the very nature of the self. You don't see awareness, and awareness doesn't see you. Instead, awareness is what you are. The two are one and the same.

The other way to address the desire to see awareness is to realize that awareness isn't the kind of thing that can be seen. It's not like a color or sound. If you could notice awareness the way you notice a color or sound, then it too would have to be an arising object. And what would this object appear to? For it to be an object, it would still need something to appear *to*. So the need to see awareness would recur again and again.

What makes witnessing awareness so prominent in the direct path isn't that it's an observed object. Instead, its prominence is based on the insight that observed objects can't appear unless they appear to witnessing awareness. Witnessing awareness is the formal and experiential requirement for there to be any appearances at all. This necessity is the basis of its always-already character.

In other words, the investigator's demand to see awareness is based on a misunderstanding of how the direct path characterizes awareness in the first place. The more clearly this is seen, the weaker will be the demand to "see" witnessing awareness.

Deconstructing Awareness Prematurely

It can seem that the direct path is all about deconstruction. It seems to be all about reducing everything to awareness. Feeling the flow of this reductive momentum, students often wish to reduce awareness to something as well, so as not to be stuck with awareness.

Although the direct path doesn't leave you stuck with awareness, it also doesn't reduce awareness to anything. There's no need. When you realize the world, the body, and the mind are nothing other than awareness, there's no need for further deconstruction. Awareness doesn't stick around as an unwanted leftover. Having done its job, it departs the scene in a gracious manner (for several examples, see chapter 9).

The urge to get rid of awareness is most often felt when people come to the direct path from other spiritual paths that don't use notions of global awareness as prominent tools. Or people may not resonate with the idea of global awareness in the first place. But even though awareness is a prominent tool in the direct path, its touch is light and loving. It's never present any longer than it's needed. There's no need to get rid of it.

Bodily Contractions

Sometimes events "in the body," such as contractions in the stomach, chest, neck, or shoulders, can make you feel like an individual entity again. In everyday terms, feelings of indignation, fear, or anger are usually accompanied by muscular contractions, as well as by judgments about how some situation will affect your interests in the future. In direct-path terms, all of these phenomena are arisings that appear spontaneously to brilliant, clear awareness.

In fact, after you investigate the body, you discover it to be nothing more than thoughts and sensations appearing to awareness. You realize that the body can't be a storehouse in which things happen. In fact, the various kinds of sensory input aren't even truly different from each other. Any difference would have to refer to the origin of the sense datum, such as the eyes, ears, hands, feet, or brain. Having realized that these supposed parts of the body are nothing more than arisings witnessed by awareness, you have no basis to believe that phenomena are objectively different from each other. Without a truly existent body or mind, these differentiations don't carry the same charge of reality that they do in the everyday sense.

This realization allows you to understand that the body doesn't truly contract. No arising has the ability to prove that your nature is a physical body. A contraction-arising is like a pain-arising—it has no special meaning in and of itself. It's not even truly a "contraction-arising." It's nothing but awareness. Anything gets a name only from some other arising that provides a name. In direct experience, there *is* no contraction.

Because the body doesn't contract, it doesn't contract into a personal entity. What you really are is the clear, open awareness that illuminates these appearances. Realizing that the body doesn't contract and isn't physical brings up a blissful sense of freedom. This freedom has joyful effects throughout the rest of your inquiry. The rest of your inquiry is accelerated because you no longer think of the mind in physical terms, as though the mind has subconscious subterranean regions within it. Instead, everything is revealed as clarity in an immediate, present way. When you don't physicalize these non-physical phenomena, you see through them much more quickly.

Of course, the fact that you realize the body and the mind are arisings in awareness doesn't necessarily reverse your everyday actions. It doesn't mean you should start avoiding physicians, massage therapists, and exercise! Those phenomena are also spontaneous arisings and don't need to be shunned or outlawed. The change is more subtle. Everyday language and everyday actions are sweetened, lightened, and clarified. They arise spontaneously without the heaviness of belief or metaphysical investment.

For more on the direct path, the body, and bodily enlightenment, see chapter 7, "The Opaque Witness."

Clarity, Transparency, and Sweetness

After you see through your sticking points, everything about awareness will become lighter and clearer. Witnessing awareness will be transparent when you no longer feel, even implicitly, that awareness has any psychological or physical properties. The less you think awareness performs a set of functions, the less limited you'll feel. When you no longer feel that awareness has mind-like properties or functions, then the more awareness will feel like your vast, clear, spacious home. When it no longer feels as if awareness is doing anything, you'll no longer think that it *is* anything. This spontaneous clarification will continue until the witnessing awareness is transparent.

With the transparency of witnessing awareness, you'll uncover a global sweetness. This isn't the sweetness of a pleasant feeling or emotion. It's much deeper than that. It's sweetness as the source and character of all arisings. No arising can block or cover up this sweetness, because the sweetness is what all arisings are made of. Your entire field of experience will become pervaded by sweetness. It'll be there during arisings, between arisings, and beyond arisings.

Experience will be beautiful, open, loving, flowing, and expansive. There'll be no suffering, boredom, or loneliness. Gone will be the older gestalt in which the objective world seemed to have the duty of catering to your separate self. When the witness is transparent, you won't feel as if appearances can possibly come from another source. (Where would that be?) You won't feel that there are unseen or non-appearing appearances. Experience will yield no basis for separation and nothing apart from your very self. Appearances will no longer feel as though they carry identification as "thoughts" or "feelings" or anything else. Appearances won't feel caused, and they won't feel linked to other arisings in causal or referential ways. There'll be no hierarchy among appearances. Appearances won't seem to be ranked or ordered in any way. No appearance will feel closer to awareness than any other. No appearance will feel more privileged or more representative of awareness. Awareness won't seem to look a certain way. This equanimity among appearances is why awareness is likened to unconditional love. Unconditional love allows all, and unconditional love blocks nothing from appearing.

You won't even have to think in terms of "appearances" or "arisings." Your allegiance to your favorite spiritual path will begin to feel more a matter of appreciation and less a matter of a unique route to truth. Even if you participate in a spiritual path, your engagement will be celebratory, not oriented toward seeking.

The Beginning of Dissolution

The onset of transparency sets the stage for the spontaneous dissolution of the witness. There's no telling how long the dissolution will take. There's a wonderful irony in this: it no longer matters! By the time you're at a point where the witness is able to dissolve, you'll no longer care whether it does indeed dissolve. You'll be at a place (which isn't a place) where there's no suffering. You'll have no doubt that the nature of all things is clarity, openness, happiness, love, and sweetness.

I discuss the dissolution in greater detail in the next chapter.

CHAPTER 9

Non-dual Realization and the End of the Witness

In the direct path, non-dual realization is the onset of the deep, experiential understanding that there's no duality anywhere. At that point, you no longer feel or experience duality, and knowledge, love, and being are as one. There's effortless wholeness, peace, presence, and love. These are not moods, thoughts, or feelings but rather the absence of anxiety, lack, and separation. For this reason, there's no need for vigilance or maintenance. There's no possibility that a separate identity will coagulate, because your realization entails the knowledge that there are no raw materials for a separate identity to be made from. There's no fear or danger of falling back or flip-flopping. There's also no feeling that experience needs to be explained in any way. There's no suspicion that "after all, *something* must be happening." There's no longer any sense that something even seems to be happening.

This is not lifeless, moribund stasis but lively, light, and free openness. Shri Atmananda used to say that this is like light "shining in its own glory." It has been likened to the *sahaja* state. This isn't a passing *samadhi* that appears to witnessing awareness; it's the end of the witness; it is establishment in your natural state.

The main factor enabling non-dual realization is the stability of the transparent witness. Once the transparent witness becomes stable, it begins to dissolve.

The Stability of the Transparent Witness

When the transparent witness is stable, you'll know without doubt that your nature is peace, happiness, and love. You'll experience

- no suffering;

- no sense that anything exists apart from awareness, or even trapped within awareness;

- no sense that anything is *non*-existent, because the very concept of "exists" will have lost its sense;

- no sense that there are multiple witnessing awarenesses;

- no sense of separation; and

- no sense that something is missing, even a hoped-for future state of non-dual realization.

Even so, according to the gestalt of the transparent witness, there'll still seem to be appearances that arise and subside. In my own journey, I used to think of these appearances as making a "serial stream." I definitely seemed to be witnessing them, and they definitely seemed to be rising and falling. But they didn't represent anything beyond themselves. I didn't feel that they were caused by anything. It was just a way that I was informally describing appearance and experience. In the midst of the sweetness that was the nature of the witness, there was no trace of suffering. There were no periods of forgetting or backsliding. There was no contraction into a "person." For me, this gestalt of the transparent witness was spontaneous, effortless, and blissful, and it lasted for about a year.

During that year, I noticed the gestalt beginning to dissolve. I felt less and less like there were appearances. I felt less of a separation between appearance and witness. And even then, the separation carried no charge. It didn't signify anything. I didn't feel as if any spiritual attainment or spiritual state was hanging in the balance. The subject/object distinction felt less and less noticeable, but it didn't disappear altogether.

In addition to this slow dissolution, I was warmly and lovingly curious about it. It wasn't a matter of happiness but perhaps a philosopher's curiosity. Why was there even the faintest trace of the subtle dualities of rising/falling and subject/object? This didn't seem like the non-dual reality that I'd read about in some of the more advanced Advaitic texts. I felt absolutely no urgency about the matter. Nothing felt pressing, but when I thought about my experience and tried to put it into words, it didn't seem like "One without a second." So for these rather abstract reasons, I began to inquire into the situation. I'll return to this below.

Why the Transparent Witness Dissolves

When the gestalt of the transparent witness has stabilized, you no longer feel separate from anything. Nothing feels as if it exists or abides separately or apart from what you know yourself to be: the awareness that's the nature of all. Because of your inquiries, discoveries, and living experience, your previous gestalt no longer makes sense. That gestalt was a conceptual scheme that interpreted the world as though there were separate things existing apart from you. Now, you no longer feel that anything is missing. You don't feel finite, localized, or limited in any way; you don't interpret arisings as signals of anything beyond themselves; you don't feel as if anything is missing or non-existent; you don't feel that anything is separate from you; and you don't think of awareness as the kind of thing that can exist in multiple places.

Once the transparent witness is stable, it begins to dissolve. There are two important reasons behind this. One reason is pragmatic and pedagogical, having to do with the direct path's nuanced approach to objects and arisings. The witness model is a *prakriya*, or "teaching model." The direct path doesn't insist upon the witness as a truly real thing. The direct path is non-dogmatic about this teaching. The idea is that the witness teaching should be able to do its work in deconstructing the notion of "objective things existing apart from awareness," but without erecting another rigidly held notion in its place.

For example, consider the direct path's wording. When discussing how no orange is found apart from an orange color, the direct path isn't saying that *the orange really is an arising*. If the orange were really an arising in awareness, then "arisings" would have to be objective existents that serve as the basis for things like oranges and tables and bodies. But the way the direct path talks about oranges and arisings is more nuanced. The direct path says that the orange is *nothing more than arisings*. In other words, in experiential terms, there's nothing about an orange that "arisings-talk" can't account for. We don't need to presume that oranges or arisings are anything more than arisings in awareness. We can account completely for our impressions of "orangeness" by inquiring into our experiences of "arisingness." There's no need to think of oranges as objective existents.

And after the gestalt of the transparent witness dissolves, even the notion of "arisingness" doesn't make sense as a lastingly true account. An arising is just a more subtle version of an orange. So the orange can't really be an arising.

The other reason why the transparent witness, once stable, begins to dissolve is that you no longer need it. It was a gestalt with a pragmatic purpose. Its purpose was to help you realize that you don't need to presume objectivity or separation in order to account for your experience. Experience doesn't need these notions.

The entire notion of "arisings in awareness" has meaning only when distinguished from "objects that are more real or substantial than arisings." That's a dichotomy that the realist or representationalist gestalt presumes to be true. These two ideas—"arisings in awareness" and "objects that are more real or substantial than arisings"—depend on each other. When it stops seeming as if it's your experience that there are objects that are more real or substantial than arisings, then the idea of arisings in awareness will stop making sense. That is, it'll turn out that you don't need to presume, even provisionally, that there are arisings or appearances. The arisings model will make less and less sense as a convincing description of your experience. What seemed to be your experience and best explanation—that arisings are happening—will begin to lose strength and conviction.

And when the arisings notion starts to make less sense, so will the very idea of witnessing awareness. Arisings versus that which sees them—these are two other ideas that need each other. If it no longer seems that there really are arisings, it'll no longer seem that there really is a witnessing awareness to which they appear. Having done its job, the witness will dissolve.

When the witness fades away, according to Shri Atmananda, we remain as "pure Consciousness," which is consciousness or awareness without the superimposition of the witnessing function.

When the perceived disappears, my perceivership also ceases and I remain as pure Consciousness.[64]

This is what the direct path calls "non-dual realization," or the *sahaja* state.

The Collapse—Inquiring into the Witness

Sometimes people are curious about the witness and think it's an unnecessary imposition. After all, many other paths don't have a notion like witnessing awareness. There are also people who, hearing that at the end of the direct path the witness dissolves or collapses, get the idea to deconstruct it at the very beginning and save time. But they won't reach their goal that way. The witness is an extremely important tool of inquiry. If you deconstruct it too soon, you'll lose access to this tool. You'll still feel like a mind in a body, and you'll be stuck without one of the direct path's sharpest tools to help you inquire into your sense of separation.

So when would be the right time to deconstruct it? Actually, you don't need to deconstruct it at all. Sooner or later it'll dissolve on its own. The "right time" would be after the transparent witness is stable. There's no need to rush. In fact, the more importance you place on deconstructing witnessing awareness, the more likely it is that the transparent witness isn't yet your experience. It dissolves most easily when it seems the least important.

In my own case of direct path–style inquiry, the witness was very stable for many months. There was no suffering, no standing as the body or mind, and no feeling that there was hidden objectivity anywhere. I never wondered about other minds or other awarenesses. I had an occasional but diminishing sense that there were spontaneous arisings, such as a rich and blissful stream of "now," "now," "now."

Perhaps because I was trained as a philosopher and I love to look into these things, I did wonder about the structure itself. The seer and the seen. I felt a warm and benevolent wonder about this gestalt not being fully "non-dual." Why was there even the most subtle sense of rising and falling? Why was there a vague sense of distinction between the appearance and the "awareness-that-I-am" to which it appeared? Nothing important depended on this. It was more like a fascinating technical puzzle that was becoming less and less fascinating as time went on.

After a few months, I began to look into this issue, the subtle dichotomy I felt between appearances and witnessing awareness. I actually asked a few teachers. They did their best to be helpful. But their guidance didn't chip away at the subtle dualism I felt was intrinsic to the witness-gestalt. The most frequent answer was along these lines: "Arisings arise from awareness. They subside back into awareness. Therefore they are nothing but awareness. There is nothing else for them to be made of. They are already awareness." This was logical as far as it went, but I felt I knew this already. I felt sure there was a deeper way of seeing that would collapse the very subtle dualistic model itself.

So I began to look into the witness model itself. I examined it in the same way that I had looked into so many other objects. The witness model began to implode, as the whole idea of arisings made less and less sense.

I began to see arisings as analogous to other objects. The logic of inquiry seemed similar. We don't directly experience arisings *as* arisings. They don't come self-labeled: "Hi, I'm an arising!" It's only a later arising that claims that there was a previous arising. But by the time the claim appears, the other arising to which it's referring isn't in evidence. Evidence is never directly present. This failure of direct evidence also happens with memory, reference, and causality. In these cases, one arising makes a claim about another arising. But that other arising is never around to verify the claim. So it dawned on me: there's no direct experience of arisings in the first place. We never have any direct experience of two arisings (or more). This includes no direct experience of two simultaneous arisings, as well as no direct experience of successive arisings one after the other. Simultaneity and succession are only concepts. By this time, I had seen through the claims of concepts.

My inquiry went like this: "Okay, so there isn't direct evidence of two arisings. How about one? Maybe everything is one big arising, slightly separate from awareness." I wondered whether the "one big arising" notion could account for the slight duality I seemed to feel about the witness model.

Well, if everything were only one big arising, it would have to be an arising that never subsided. But that didn't accord with my experience. Along with the witness model, I did seem to experience a coming and going. I seemed to feel the coming and going, but the idea of witnessed arisings was making no sense.

But I'm glad I did contemplate the single-arising idea. It helped me realize that the very notion of "arising" requires that there be many arisings. The idea of one big arising in the history of all experience just didn't make sense. It made no sense to think of something as an "arising" if it was supposed to be alone in the universe. So for me, the very model of arisings collapsed. It made no sense that there were two or more arisings. And it made no sense that there was only one arising. For me, this very logic of the witness model collapsed the witness model. It just stopped making sense. It stopped seeming like my experience. Even the sense of comings and goings stopped. It had been linked to idea of arisings. The collapse of the model took all its parts with it. "Comings and goings," "arisings," "appearances," a "witness to which they appear"—none of these were my experience anymore.

Non-dual Realization

This is how it happens in the direct path: If you come this far with direct path–style inquiry, the witness either dissolves or collapses. It doesn't matter. In either case, you've already realized non-separation, openness, and happiness from the transparent witness. According to the direct path, when the witness collapses, it collapses into pure consciousness, our true nature. This is consciousness without the additional function of appearance being attributed to it. In the theoretical sense and the experiential sense, there's no seeming appearance or disappearance. There are no experienced dualities at all.

Whatever the transparent witness feels like, the post-witness feeling is more open and unrestricted. To put it, very inaccurately, into more familiar terms, the experience of witnessing awareness is like the freedom of walking on the moon, where you weigh only 16 percent as much as you weigh on Earth. But the post-witness experience is like floating in space. There's no friction or constraint at all.

Limits can't even be imagined. Experience defies verbalization. Life is lived in happiness, love, and celebration. If there has been an ethical component in your life, you'll see deeper and more spontaneous integration of this approach. Saying all this is in one sense saying too much and in another sense not saying enough.

Then What?

Again, speaking in an everyday sense, there's usually a stabilizing process, in which the body and the mind align themselves to this new freedom. Some people begin teaching or forming communities to be with others of a similar mind-set. I became very interested in one facet of stabilization, one having to do with speech and thought. For several months after the witness collapsed, I had a feeling of having lost my language. To speak seriously about ethics, bodies, minds, stabilization, and communities seemed to amount to taking a viewpoint, and that felt odd. It also felt as though there was no precedent in the official direct-path vocabulary. This sounds paradoxical, but it's quite natural. I discuss in the next chapter how this can happen. I think of it as an example of joyful irony.

CHAPTER 10

After Awareness—
The End of the Path

After the transparent witness becomes your experiential gestalt, it'll have done its job. The witness and arisings will begin to dissolve. If you inquire into the "witness versus arisings" issue in a benevolent and dispassionate way, you may experience a quicker collapse. Either way, it won't matter, and you'll no longer feel that appearances or arisings are happening. You'll no longer feel as if witnessing is happening. In terms of the direct path, the dualities of subject/object and one/many are the most subtle of all, because they're involved in all other dualities. You can deconstruct all the other dualities (which is the job of the witness teaching) and still be left with these. With the dissolution of the witness, you'll no longer experience these dualities.

Officially, the direct path explains this by saying that you've reached pure consciousness, *sahaja samadhi*, "light shining in its own glory." The teaching officially stops there. It's a perfectly acceptable end point from the perspective of the direct path. After all, what kind of teaching would be necessary beyond that point? What kind of teaching would be possible?

But I'd like to talk about this in a more personal way. What happened in my case was bizarre and unpredictable.

I remember the day the collapse happened. I had just come back from a weeklong retreat, and I was happily and dreamily inquiring into the whole issue of arisings appearing to awareness. It felt a bit gappish—that distinction between subject and object. After I did some contemplation of the whole mechanism of appearance and witnessing, the gestalt disappeared. It was as though the gaps were filled in. Subject and object didn't feel separate anymore. They didn't feel like anything at all. This wasn't a temporary interruption in the flow of arisings, as in a "zone" or trance experience. It was a case where this subtle dualistic kind of experience didn't apply anymore. It was no longer my experience, and it didn't make sense as an explanation either.

For the next few days, I realized that this was what is taught as pure consciousness—consciousness or awareness without an object. This is the official direct-path teaching. I could see its appeal. But as time went on, I began to feel as if "pure consciousness" was saying too much. I felt no need to conceptualize in these terms. "Pure consciousness" felt meaningful only if there was something to contrast it with. But I didn't have anything to serve as contrast.

Communication

As I mentioned at the beginning of this book, a lot of my reflections are about communication, not just about direct-path insights. In the late 1990s, I noticed that in communicating, even sometimes in thinking, I began to feel as though I had lost my language. The vocabulary of the direct path no longer seemed to be closer to my experience than any other. It was a wonderful and dizzying feeling. It came up a lot in discussions with others. Many times in discussions about non-dualism, or about experience, identity, knowledge, and freedom, people are interested to hear "how things are" or "how it is for you?" I felt that I was without words. It felt as though anything I said would be a contraction into a position of some sort, which didn't feel real or sincere. I didn't know what to say. No matter what I thought or spoke about, it was like a little joker character was peering out from behind the words, saying "Not really!" At the time I was participating in a few e-mail discussion lists with non-dual themes. I did my share of non-dual babbling, but I didn't really talk about this strange phenomenon.

Over the years, I had studied many philosophies and paths. I was aware of a variety of vocabularies. And now, unless I was explicitly playing the role of a direct-path participant, none of these vocabularies seemed preferable in terms of truth or accuracy. When I was left to myself, experience didn't show up as anything at all. There was nothing strictly true or strictly false to say about it.

Not Even Consciousness

After several months, I encountered something that served as a kind of confirmation. I came across the privately circulated commentary on *Ashtavakra Samhita* attributed to Shri Atmananda. *Ashtavakra Samhita* is a lyrical expression of the joys of self-knowledge. In his comments on verse 18:95, the author answers the question "What exists?" The answer is as if from the highest perspective. His expression in this passage is both palpably joyful and nonreferential. Basically, he says that we can't say anything at all. At this level, if we try to say something, we'll just get dizzy. Everything is paradoxical. We can't even say that it's consciousness or that anything exists! It's a joyful, effusive case of saying without saying.

When I read this, I felt that I was on the right track. I felt that the direct path had helped me find freedom, including freedom from itself. The author's comments seemed to communicate my present insight more fully than the official teachings of the direct path. It was odd, because the official teachings had helped foster this insight! So this "not even consciousness" insight seemed like a hidden teaching. In fact, I can see why it might be purposely withheld. Students who encounter it too soon could take it literally and reject the very idea of consciousness before the idea has had a chance to work.

After reading that privately circulated commentary, I started looking more widely for evocative articulations similar to it. I looked outside the direct path. I looked to both the East and the West. I had long been fascinated by the whole area of spirituality, thought, and language, and I had a feeling that there were many more ways to engage this area.

One of the most helpful things I found was Richard Rorty's idea of the "liberal ironist."[65] Richard Rorty (1931–2007) was a well-known antifoundationalist philosopher in the Western academic tradition. For most of his forty-year career, Rorty challenged the ideas of philosophical certainties and metaphysical foundations. A metaphysical foundation corresponds roughly to what I've been calling "objectivity" in this book. For Rorty, "liberals" are those who wish to avoid cruelty to others, and "ironists" are those who face up to how their most cherished beliefs and desires have no objective grounds.

Joyful Irony

Rorty's work in this area spoke deeply to me, so I adapted his political, antimetaphysical notion of the liberal ironist for spiritual purposes, conceiving the "joyful ironist." The joyful ironist has found loving, openhearted happiness without dogmatism. The "joy" comes from love and happiness, often gained as a result of inquiry, insight, or devotion. The "irony" has to do with a radical relationship to conceptuality and language, as explained below.

Normally, we have a vocabulary (which includes a conceptual scheme) that we feel best expresses the truth of things. Rorty calls this our "final vocabulary." For those on a spiritual path, the path itself may become their final vocabulary. For others, their final vocabulary may be popular science. Whatever their final vocabulary, people believe it's better than other vocabularies at representing reality accurately or correctly. Perhaps they believe it's grounded in or guaranteed by reality itself. A final vocabulary might not even be recognized as a vocabulary by those using it. It might just feel like "the truth." This could be called the metaphysical approach to conceptuality and language.

In joyful irony, we continue to use language, and we usually continue to have a final vocabulary, but with a difference. We no longer have a model in which there's language on one side and reality on the other, and our vocabulary points to reality. In fact, the very idea of a strict dualism between language and reality stops making sense. It's not that one side creates or reduces to the other. Rather, the idea of drawing a line to separate them loses the sense it had before. The issue no longer has any metaphysical importance. No vocabulary seems as if it does the best job of drawing such a line. (For more on this nonreferential approach to language, see chapter 3, "The Language of Joyful Irony.")

The joy and the irony must work together. If you're joyful without being ironic, you'll still have attachments to your own views of things. And if you're ironic without being joyful, you may be bitter, cynical, sarcastic, and pessimistic. Heartfelt wisdom includes both sides. Joy adds love to irony. Irony adds clarity to joy.

Joyful Irony, not Relativism or Neutrality

As a joyful ironist, you don't need to maintain a posture of neutrality between vocabularies or ways of life. Joyful irony isn't an artificial stance or a position that needs maintenance. It's more as if the demand has fallen away for foundations in thought, communication, and ways of life.

You're free to have resonances. You can have a favorite or final vocabulary. An ironist's final vocabulary isn't grounded; it's just the vocabulary that he or she feels most comfortable with. If metaphysicians ask me, for example, to support my particular choice of vocabulary by citing objective grounds, I won't be able to answer. My final vocabulary feels appealing and resonant. If the metaphysicians keep pushing me to justify my vocabulary, I can only respond that it takes me as far as I can go before having to resort to grunts, gestures, and attempts to change the subject. But of course, as a joyful ironist, I realize that the metaphysicians can't give objective grounds for their choices of vocabularies either. An important difference, however, is that I've looked into this particular issue and am quite happy about it.

Classic relativism is different from joyful irony. Relativists' final vocabulary is relativism. Relativism usually says something like

"The truth of vocabulary X is relative to Y," where Y is culture, history, social factors, or other variables. Relativism is an attempt at a broader, higher view, a view that's free from local or cultural specifics.

So if you're a relativist, you'll try to be neutral about other vocabularies. You'll believe that to deeply engage in a form of spirituality, you need to feel that this path tells the objective truth about things. If you feel that it doesn't tell the metaphysical truth about things, then you shouldn't engage it seriously. You'll hold back and try to maintain neutrality.

This is because most relativism[66] is still metaphysical at heart. Unlike joyful irony, most relativism sees itself as a true truth. It gets caught up in the unintended irony of attachment to its own view, as though it hasn't taken note of the joyful ironist's slogan, "Joyful irony begins at home."

But if you're a joyful ironist, you don't need to do any of this maneuvering or posturing. You're free to embrace a vocabulary as deeply as you want. Your metaphysical yearning has become dismantled, and you don't need to defend against it. You don't have to scale back your engagement in a way of life in order to maintain neutrality. You don't have to hold back or attain a posture of ultimate non-involvement. Not matter how deeply you get involved, you won't be able to take a vocabulary as a grounded truth. Most significantly, this begins with your own favorite vocabulary.

Speaking for myself, I can say that freedom from the objectivist, metaphysical gestalt has made me interested in other vocabularies, views, and cultures. I've always liked these kinds of topics.

You may go a different way. As a joyful ironist, you may or may not develop pluralistic interests. In either case, you won't be able to cling to your favorite path as true and look down on other paths as less than true. These side effects of true belief will simply not be possible for you. (The more you've experienced people communicating in snobbish or exclusivist ways about spiritual matters, the more you'll be able to savor the openness I'm discussing here.)

After Awareness

For joyful ironists, "after awareness" doesn't signal a rejection of awareness. It doesn't mean that awareness has ceased to exist or never existed. It doesn't mean that there's a higher truth on the horizon. Rather, it's a joyfully ironic approach to awareness. Awareness may be loved, appreciated, or engaged, but there's no attachment to it. It's not something that we insist is everyone's reality or truth whether they know it or not.

There's a wonderfully fitting parallel between the phrases "joyful irony" and "after awareness." The "joy" comes from awareness, and the "after" comes from irony.

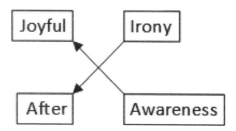

That is, the "after" doesn't refer to a point in time but serves as a metaphor for the ironic approach. The "awareness" doesn't refer to the core reality of the universe but serves as a metaphor for the freedom and joy that have flourished with the help of this teaching.

For the joyful ironist, the teaching of awareness has enabled freedom, love, and happiness. And even though awareness is a major element in the direct path, it's no longer a matter of truth or reality for the joyful ironist. The conceptual structure that places so much importance on these categories has been deconstructed. So the joyful ironist is unable to say things like the following and mean them in the metaphysical sense: "When you say 'God,' you're really referring to consciousness." "The true meaning of all spiritual teachings is awareness as the one reality." If statements like this ever seemed appealingly true, they no longer do. For the joyful ironist, it's as if "awareness" is always in quotes. In fact, it's as if *all* words are always in quotes!

This lighthearted approach to life doesn't push you into a stupefied, mute, inactive, or nihilistic corner. Quite the contrary. You discover new sources of energy, enthusiasm, and creativity coming from every direction. It's exhilarating!

The End of the Path

In the phrase "the end of the path," the word "end" has several senses. In one sense, "end" means "purpose." The purpose of this path is peace, love, happiness, and integration in life. In another sense, "end" refers to a final state.

If you feel a deep intuitive connection with the awareness teaching, the direct path's view of things might seem like the best and truest explanation of experience anywhere. You may even feel odd when participating in everyday talk. For example, if you tell your doctor that you've been having headaches, you may wonder: *Am I somehow violating non-dual truth by saying this? Because, really, who is there to have a headache? Isn't the head just a family of sensations and thoughts appearing to awareness?*

There's no violation here. With experience and with some effective mentoring, you can shift effectively back and forth between the direct-path view and your everyday view. The direct path's view will probably seem like the more profound truth, and that's okay. Over much of the course of the direct path, it doesn't impede your progress to see the direct path as telling the metaphysical truth about the world. The issue of metaphysical truth is looked into sooner or later, and the feeling of needing objective metaphysical grounding dissolves.

The purpose of the direct path's non-dual inquiry is to deconstruct your allegiance to the separate, objective existence of the self and objects that make up the mind, the body, and the world. Openhearted mentoring and communication can prevent you from becoming rigid and dogmatic in your investigation. (When these interactions are loving and effective, they're conveyed in an open, generous, loving way that communicates inclusion. Effective spiritual communication doesn't encourage chauvinistic attitudes toward alternate views.)

And then, when you reach "self-knowledge" or "the dissolution of the witness" or "non-dual realization," you won't inherit dogmatism as part of the package. Joyful irony will flourish.

The freedom you'll discover *through* the path includes freedom *from* the path. In both senses of the word, this is the "end" of the path.

Acknowledgments

I wish to thank Kavitha Chinnaiyan, Steve Diamond, Nick Diggins, and Neil Jalaldeen for their suggestions in the completion of this book. These are some difficult topics to talk about, but you helped smooth the way. Any remaining infelicities are due to yours truly.

Notes

1: See verse 17 in his *Upadesa Saram*. (Bangalore, India: Ramana Maharshi Center for Learning, 1984)

2: See my answer to the realist critique on p. 13 and in *The Direct Path: A User Guide* (Non-Duality Press, 2009) chap. 7.

3: See the definition of *tattvopadesha* in Nitya Tripta, *Notes on Spiritual Discourses of Shri Atmananda* (Salisbury, UK: Non-Duality Press & Stillness Speaks, 2009), vol. 3, p. 250.

4: *Atma Darshan* was first published in India in 1945. *Atma Nirvriti* was first published in India in 1951. The two were published in a double edition by Advaita Publishers in Austin, Texas, in 1983.

5: In *Atma Darshan*, see the preface, p. 2. See also chaps. 2, 5, and 18. In *Atma Nirvriti*, see especially chap. 3. See also the essays at the end, "World" and "Witness." See also chaps. 6, 13, and 18.

6: Platform Sutra quotes are from pp. 130 and 132, respectively, of *The Platform Sutra of the Sixth Patriarch*, trans. Philip Yampolsky (New York: Columbia University Press, 1967).

7: See *The Direct Path: A User Guide*, pt. 2, "The Container Metaphor in Western Culture."

8: Adi Shankaracharya, who lived in India in the early 8th century CE, was the most prominent philosopher and teacher in the tradition of Advaita Vedanta. See his *Tattva Bodha*, verses 1–7, and *Vivekachudamani*, verses 19ff.

9: See Jeffrey Hopkins' *Meditation on Emptiness*, rev. ed. (Boston, MA: Wisdom Publications, 1996), pp. 282–83.

10: The Dalai Lama and Howard Cutler, *The Art of Happiness in a Troubled World* (New York: Random House, 2009), p. 331.

11: Sandra Heber-Percy, *Awakening to Consciousness* (Bangalore, India: Sai Tower Press, 2008), p. 190.

12: As a matter of fact, Heber-Percy's book (which supplied the passage about noninvolvement of the "Sage") also devotes several adulatory chapters each to Sathya Sai Baba and Ramesh Balsekar. Both of these men were the subject of allegations of sexual and financial misconduct. The allegations were current for many years before 2008, when the book was published.

13: The idea of ethical action as involving skills goes back to the ancient Greek philosophers. For an accessible modern review, see Julia Annas, *The Morality of Happiness* (Oxford University Press, 1995), p. 67ff.

14: Nitya Tripta, *Notes on Spiritual Discourses of Shri Atmananda*, vol. 2, p. 14. *Notes*, compiled by Nitya Tripta, contains dialogues from Shri Atmananda from 1950 to 1959. All references to *Notes* are to the three-volume set published by Non-Duality Press and Stillness Speaks in 2009.

15: See https://www.appa.edu/code.htm.

16: Originally published by HarperCollins Press in 1999.

17: Not his real name.

18: Even though this chapter is in and about English, I've found that the insights apply to other languages as well.

19: See *Atma Darshan*, p. 1.

20: See Swami Sivananda, *Vedanta for Beginners* (Rishikesh, India: Divine Life Society, 1941), and Bimal Krishna Matilal, *The Word and the World: India's Contribution to the Study of Language* (New York: Oxford University Press, 1990).

21: Nitya Tripta, *Notes*, vol. 1, p. 80.

22: See experiments 17, 18, and 19 in *The Direct Path: A User Guide*.

23: The most fully developed presentation of the coherence theory I have seen is from Brand Blanshard, *Nature of Thought* (London: George Allen and Unwin, 1939), chap. XXVI.

24: Nitya Tripta, *Notes*, vol. 3, p. 215.

25: Nitya Tripta, *Notes*, vol. 3, p. 216. An *uttamadhikari* (*uttama* means "highest") is an aspirant with the highest qualifications for self-knowledge.

26: Nitya Tripta, *Notes*, vol. 3, p. 28.

27: Nitya Tripta, *Notes*, vol. 1, p. 206.

28: Nitya Tripta, *Notes*, vol. 2, p. 195, emphasis added.

29: Nitya Tripta, *Notes*, vol. 2, p. 196.

30: Nitya Tripta, *Notes*, vol. 1, p. 181.

31: Nitya Tripta, *Notes*, vol. 3, pp. 141–42.

32: Nitya Tripta, *Notes*, vol. 3, pp. 215–16.

33: Nitya Tripta, *Notes*, vol. 2, p. 197.

34: *Atmananda Tattwa Samhita: The Direct Approach to Truth as Expounded by Shri Atmananda* was recorded between 1951 and 1959. Its first copyright was 1973. It was reprinted in 1983 and 1991 in Austin, Texas, by Advaita Publishers.

35: *Ashtavakra Samhita* is an ancient scripture from Advaita Vedanta. It consists of a dialogue between the sage Ashtavakra and King Janaka. Swami Nityaswarupananda (1899–1992) translated *Ashtavakra Samhita* into English over the period 1929 to 1931. Shri Atmananda wrote a commentary based on Swami Nityaswarupananda's translation. As far as I know, the document containing *Ashtavakra Samhita* and Shri Atmananda's commentary was never published; it was only circulated privately.

36: The title page gives the title as *Notes on Spiritual Discourses of Shri Atmananda*. Below that, it reads "taken by Nitya Tripta."

37: See especially 10:IV, 10:XXV, and 12:III–VI.

38: See *Notes*, vol. 1, p. 65. *Vritti* is a kind of thought wave or functional modification of the mind. *Vidya-vritti* is a modification of the mind that results in clarity or right knowledge. *Viveka-vritti* is a modification of the mind that results in discrimination between the permanent and the temporary, the true and the false, and so on.

39: Direct quotation of a few lines would be very helpful here. But due to the extremely strict interpretation of copyright law on the part of his publisher, I'm unable to quote from any works with Shri Atmananda's byline.

40: The version of *Ashtavakra Samhita* used for Shri Atmananda's commentary is based on Swami Nityaswarupananda's translation into English. Shri Atmananda's version is largely consistent with Swami Nityaswarupananda's second edition, which was published in 1953 by Advaita Ashrama, Mayavati, Almora, Himalayas (first edition c. 1940). If Shri Atmananda used the second edition, his own commentary would have been completed between 1953 and his own passing in 1959. All references are to the second edition.

41: p. vi.

42: p. v.

43: See Nitya Tripta, *Notes*, vol. 3, pp. 237–38, for a discussion of *Atma Darshan* and *Atma Nirvriti*.

44: Nitya Tripta, *Notes*, vol. 2, p. 3.

45: See for example verse 1.3.28 of the *Brihadaranyaka Upanishad*, which is an invocation to lead us from the unreal to the real, from darkness to light, and from death to immortality. By following this verse and its associated teaching, are we *really* trying to accomplish something that isn't already accomplished? I don't wish to critique or endorse Shri Atmananda's account of the Upanishadic methods. I suspect that a sufficiently nuanced reading of this verse may amount to just as much directness as Shri Atmananda attributes to his own process.

46: Nitya Tripta, *Notes*, vol. 1, p. 126.

47: Nitya Tripta, *Notes*, vol. 1, p. xx.

48: Nitya Tripta, *Notes*, vol. 3, p. 215.

49: A state reached through meditation in which there are no objects appearing— all that's present is awareness itself.

50: See *The Direct Path: A User Guide*, pt. 1, for more information.

51: See experiments 11, 12a, and 12b in *The Direct Path: A User Guide*.

52: This teaching posits awarenesses for the eye, the ear, the nose, the tongue, and the body. They're called "sense direct perceivers," and there are many of each, even within the same person. Each sense direct perceiver is said to come about from the meeting of an object and a sense power. The Geluk order follows the epistemological categories given in Sautrantika Buddhism. For more information, see Lati Rinpochay, *Mind in Tibetan Buddhism*, ed. and trans. Elizabeth Napper (Ithaca, NY: Snow Lion Publications, 1980), p. 71.

53: Thomas Metzinger is quite popular as a neurophilosopher and as a popularizer of neuroscience. His more recent books, such as *The Ego Tunnel: The Science of the Mind and the Myth of the Self* (New York: Basic Books, 2009) and *Being No One: The Self-Model Theory of Subjectivity* (Cambridge, MA: MIT Press, 2003), even have a soteriological edge. The most extreme form of reductionism that I'm familiar with has been argued by John W. Bickle Jr. of Mississippi State University's Philosophy and Religion Department. See his "Reducing Mind to Molecular Pathways: Explicating the Reductionism Implicit in Current Cellular and Molecular Neuroscience," *Synthese* 151 (2006): 411–34, or *Psychoneural Reduction: The New Wave* (Cambridge, MA: MIT Press, 1998).

54: There are other types of skepticism—for example, Pyrrhonism—that don't accept realism at all. See Greg Goode and Tomas Sander, *Emptiness and Joyful Freedom*, (Salisbury, UK: Non-Duality Press, 2013), chap. 17.

55: The senses are usually thought to include vision, hearing, smell, taste, and touch. We may even add a sixth, or intuitive, sense to the list.

56: *Tattvopadesha* refers to the logically connected presentation of all the direct-path teachings.

57: This is a kind of investigative proof-by-experience called "higher" because it's able to investigate the mind itself. Since the mind can't investigate itself (in the same sense that a knife can't cut itself), the direct path calls this kind of subtle investigation "coming from awareness," which is "higher" than the mind.

58: Judith Blackstone, "Embodied Nonduality," *Undivided: The Online Journal of Nonduality and Psychology* 1, no. 2 (May 31, 2012): p. 10. http://undivided journal.com/wp-content/uploads/2012/05/embodied nonduality.pdf.

59: Ibid., comment posted July 10, 2012, at 1:58 p.m. Permalink accessed Feb. 28, 2015: http://undividedjournal.com/2012/05/31/embodied-nonduality.

60: Scott Kiloby, "Conscious Embodiment" (2014). Permalink accessed Feb. 28, 2015: http://kiloby.com/conscious-embodiment.

61: Berkeley's most accessible book is *Three Dialogues Between Hylas and Philonous in Opposition to Sceptics and Atheists* (1713). I heartily recommend the version found on Jonathan Bennett's Early Modern Texts website (http://www.earlymoderntexts.com/assets/pdfs/berkeley1713.pdf). Professor Bennett has worked hard to update the language of Berkeley's text and make it easier to understand for the modern reader.

62: See *The Direct Path: A User Guide*, pt. 3.

63: *The Direct Path: A User Guide* contains no investigation into the subject/object distinction involving other people. If I were to add such an investigation, a good place would be in part 3 of that book, in which I discuss the mind. At that point, readers have looked into the world and also the body, discovering that the world and the body are never experienced to exist independently of awareness. And then in part 3 they get to the mind, and they see through alienating metaphors such as "the ghost in the machine." That would be a good place to look into the question of other people.

The reason I left this issue out of *The Direct Path: A User Guide* is that it's already covered under the topics of world, body, and mind. The book features investigations about objects in the world. It looks into issues of body and mind quite thoroughly. Readers get to the point where they experience themselves as awareness and not as people.

64: Nitya Tripta, *Notes*, vol. 1, p. 42.

65: See Richard Rorty, *Contingency, Irony, and Solidarity* (New York: Cambridge University Press, 1989), especially the introduction and chap. 4.

66: I say that "most" relativism is metaphysical because there are also non-metaphysical, ironic varieties of relativism. For a good example, see Ugo Zilioli, *Protagoras and the Challenge of Relativism: Plato's Subtlest Enemy* (Burlington, VT: Ashgate, 2007).

Greg Goode is known for a unique combination of penetrating insight, comfort with both Eastern and Western sources, and a down-to-earth sense of humor. He is author of *Standing as Awareness*, *The Direct Path*, and many popular articles, and coauthor of *Emptiness and Joyful Freedom*. Goode studied psychology at California State University, Long Beach, and philosophy at the University of Rochester and the University of Cologne. He became drawn to self-inquiry through the work of Brand Blanshard, George Berkeley, the Chinmaya Mission, and the Arsha Vidya Gurukulam. Goode is a member of the American Philosophical Practitioners Association (APPA), and serves as technical consultant for their peer-reviewed journal *Philosophical Practice*. He lives in New York City, where he enjoys literature, film, cycling, and spending time with his family.

Index

C

cause and effect: 158, 160

Christianity: 38-39

clarity: 4, 7, 9, 18, 29, 82, 97, 102, 105, 109, 113, 120, 125-126, 155, 158, 167, 169, 183, 193

Coherence (of the world): 162

communication: 2-3, 27, 58, 63, 68, 70, 73, 80, 90-91, 94, 180, 183, 186-187

compassion: 31, 33, 40, 44-45, 81

concentration: 22, 40, 42, 134

Conscious Embodiment (article by Scott Kiloby): 143, 195

Consciousness. See Awareness

Container (as metaphor): 25, 110, 122, 191

Contemplation: 67, 88, 91, 101-102, 106, 176, 180

critiques: 1, 23-24, 46, 49-50, 56

D

deconstruction: 1, 146, 165-166

Deep sleep. See Sleep, deep

despair: 106

devotion: 9, 43, 84, 87-88, 99, 182

Direct experience. See Experience, direct

Direct method. See Method, direct

Direct Path, The (book by Greg Goode): 66, 194

Discrimination: 41, 91, 193

Dispassion: 41

Dissolution (of the transparent witness): 20, 111, 169, 172, 179, 187

doership: 48, 160-161

Durga (Hindu deity): 43, 99

E

Ego and His Own, The: The Case of the Individual Against Authority (book by Max Stirner): 36

egolessness: 86

Embodied Nonduality (article by Judith Blackstone): 142, 195

ethics: 31-36, 38-50, 55-58, 60, 81, 178

evidence: 12-15, 23, 28, 79, 119, 127-131, 150, 152, 156, 159, 161, 176

Existence (of the world): 29, 120

Experience, direct: 6, 11-18, 23, 28, 30, 64-65, 94, 96-97, 103, 105, 112, 114, 120, 123-130, 143, 151-152, 156, 159-161, 164, 167, 176

F

Faith: 37, 42

Fifth Patriarch. See Patriarch, Fifth

Figurative language. See Language, figurative)

Forbearance: 42

G

God: 33, 38-39, 99, 118, 185

Good Samaritan: 34

gospel music: 34, 37

Guru, the: 6, 74, 83-95, 98-100

H

Hawkins, Edwin (1943-): 37

hearing: 14-17, 22, 61, 65, 116, 119, 125, 174, 194

higher reasoning: 18, 23, 91, 96, 135

Hinduism: 34

hopelessness: 106, 154

Hui-neng (Fifth Patriarch): 22

I

inference: 12, 91, 124, 130-131, 135

interpretation: 12, 74, 76, 124, 130, 137, 193

irony: 6-7, 21-22, 28, 51, 61-62, 72, 78, 80-82, 94-95, 115, 123, 158, 169, 178, 182-185, 187, 195

Q

Qualifications (for a suitable student of Vedanta): 41-46, 56, 93
quietness: 12, 101

R

Ramana Maharshi (1879-1950): 8-9, 75
Rand, Ayn (1905-1982): 36
Realism (philosophical view): 121-122, 126, 194
Realization, nondual: 1, 3, 6-8, 20, 23, 40-41, 52, 114, 142-143, 153, 156, 158, 170-171, 174, 177, 187
Realization, self: 3, 84-85, 88-93
Reasoning. *See* Higher reasoning
Relative level. *See* level, Relative
Relativism (philosophical view): 183-184, 195
reminders: 6, 8, 94, 97, 100, 102-103
Renard, Philip: 9
Representationalism (philosophical view): 62, 64-65, 79-81
Rorty, Richard (1931-2007): 81, 182, 195
Rosicricianism: —

S

Sadhana Chatushtaya. See Qualifications)
Sajaha samadhi. See Samadhi, sahaja
Samadhi, nirvikalpa: 102, 106
Samadhi, sahaja: 7, 102, 106, 170, 179
satsang: 58, 75-76
self-inquiry: 3, 6, 9-11, 13, 17-19, 22-23, 43-44, 61, 85, 87, 91, 106, 118, 154
Self-realization. *See* Realization, self
sentience: 10-11, 112, 153
Seva (Service in Hinduism): 21, 34, 43
Shakti (Hindu deity): 43
Shankaracharya, Adi (mid to late 8th century CE): 41, 191

Shiva (Hindu deity): 43, 87, 99,
Sixth Patriarch. *See* Patriarch, Sixth
sleep: 10, 106-108, 122
Sleep, deep: 106-108
Solipsism (philosophical view in which there are no other people or entities): 144
sound: 10, 14-16, 24, 65, 69, 115, 119, 124, 165
space: 61-62, 82, 109, 113, 123, 143, 147, 177
speech: 38, 44, 46, 53, 58, 63, 66, 76, 93, 141, 178
Spira, Rupert (1960 -): 9, 84
Stability (of the transparent witness): 170-171
standing as awareness: 6, 8, 97, 103-104
Stirner, Max (Johann Kaspar Schmidt, 1806-1856): 36
Sublation (a view deconstructed and incorporated into a more subtle view): 136, 138,
Swami Nityaswarupananda. *See* Nityaswarupananda, Swami
sweetness: 7, 9, 20, 44, 104, 106, 123, 125-126, 167-169, 171

T

Tattva Bodha (text by Adi Shankaracharya): 41, 191
Tattvopadesha (teaching on reality): 19, 88-89, 96, 191, 194
teaching model: 172
The Heart Opener: 8, 97, 105-106, 154, 164
The Morality of Happiness (book by Julia Annas): 53, 192
The Word and the World: India's Contribution to the Study of Language (book by Bimal Krishna Matilal): 67, 192
thoughts: 3, 11-12, 14, 17-18, 44, 53, 81, 97, 101-103, 105-106, 109, 113,